BIG CHIEF AREA CLIMBS

The Climbing Guide to the Big Chief Area, Lake Tahoe

1ST EDITION

See Page 70

Andrea Jensen on **Dogfight** 11b****. ©*Jim Kovacs Photo.*

BIG CHIEF AREA CLIMBS

The Climbing Guide to the Big Chief Area, Lake Tahoe

BY MAREK HAJEK
EDITED BY MARTY LEWIS
1ST EDITION

LAKE TAHOE AREA CLIMBING GUIDES VOL. 1

MAXIMVS PRESS

Big Chief Area Climbs 1st Edition
The Climbing Guide to the Big Chief Area, Lake Tahoe
by Marek Hajek, edited by Marty Lewis
LAKE TAHOE AREA CLIMBING GUIDES VOL. 1

Maximus Press
P.O. Box 1565
Bishop, CA 93515
Phone & Fax: 760-387-1013
E-mail: smlewis@qnet.com
http://maximuspress.com

Front Cover Photo: Dave Hatchett on **Blazing Buckets** 13b*** (1992). *©Mike Hatchett Photo.*
Back Cover Photo: The Middle Area at Big Chief. *©Pete Dronkers Photo.*

MAXIMVS PRESS

New Route Information and Comments

Please e-mail, call or send any new route information, comments, ratings, errors, or criticisms to Maximus Press. Contact information is on the previous page.

The author can be e-mailed directly at BigChiefGuide@hotmail.com. For the latest information and route updates visit maximuspress.com/bigchief.

About Climbing Guides

There are very few facts in a guidebook. Climbing guides are simply collections of personal opinions. At best the information is based on a broad consensus, but it can also be just the experience of the author or even hearsay.

The moment a guidebook comes out it begins a slow downward slide in accuracy. Holds break, routes get added, routes get removed, bolts fail, government policies change, roads close, prices go up, businesses close and acts of god occur. What you find in the real world takes precedence over anything found in a guidebook. Use your own judgement.

While most art can be easily thrown away and forgotten, the art that a first ascentionist busts out on our public lands can last for generations. So, it is important that we have the freedom to critique these creations. If you write a guidebook, you're guaranteed to ruffle some feathers. Thankfully, in this great country the freedom to express these opinions is guaranteed.

The thing to keep in mind is that guidebooks are personal, subjective works of opinion. Try not to take them too seriously. And if you want a perfect guidebook, you'll have to write it yourself!

—Marty Lewis

Mick Ryan Photo.

ACKNOWLEDGMENTS

It took eighteen months of concentrated effort to complete this guide. During this process it became apparent to me that guidebooks are not born from the efforts of one person alone but from the synergy of many selfless individuals. Many heartfelt thanks go to the following people that made a special contribution:

Pete Dronkers spent much time photographing the cliff from every possible angle. We photographed Big Chief close up, from across the valley and from an airplane to get a perspective on the routes. Pete has demonstrated tremendous photography expertise. His never-ending positive energy spurred me on during the down times. Thanks!

My wife, Trang Hajek, stood by me, endured sweltering summer heat and winter cold while belaying me as I was evaluating routes and counting bolts. Thanks for the help and of course for all the other support necessary to make this project happen.

Dave and Mike Hatchett. Dave spent time with me at Big Chief clarifying several route locations. He described some of the history behind Big Chief in the Foreword and patiently answered my questions. Mike donated a number of action photos. Dave and Mike are the Big Chief original pioneers. They put up more routes at Big Chief than anybody else. Their help and guidance during the making of this guide is greatly appreciated!

Jim Kovacs drove up to Big Chief at 6 A.M. to take action photos during soft lighting conditions for this guide. Despite his fear of heights he jumared up ropes next to several routes to get a good angle on the action photos. Many thanks for your effort and working through the fear of heights. You did a tremendous job!

Chris Kurrle and Mike McCabe fixed up a number of routes, adding bolts and anchors, developed new routes at Sawtooth Ridge and provided me with extensive feedback on quality and difficulty ratings. Chris and Mike are the modern Dave and Mike Hatchett of Sawtooth Ridge. Chris drew and donated the Sawtooth Ridge topos, wrote the Sawtooth introduction and provided quality and difficulty ratings. Bottom line, without his help, Sawtooth Ridge would not have made it into this edition. Awesome job! Many thanks for your selfless effort to improve Big Chief and help with this project!

Marty Lewis guided and encouraged me throughout this whole process. Marty has published numerous guidebooks throughout the years. His expertise in guidebook publishing is what made this book possible. Marty edited this book, drew topos, and created maps for Big Chief. I am not sure Marty knew what he was getting into when he agreed to work on this guidebook with me, away from his home area. Nevertheless, he drove up here time and time again. Thanks for sticking with it and seeing the project till the end.

Mike Ossofsky loyally supported my bolt counting, topo map creation, photography and trail improvement efforts, trip after trip. He has made more trips with me to Big Chief over the last eighteen months than anyone. Mike would typically clear the manzanita from the trail while I was taking notes for the topos. No matter how trashed we would get climbing and evaluating routes, Mike never said no when I called him the following day to go again. Much thanks!

Manuel Souza climbed a number of trees to take photographs for topo maps. He lent me his photography equipment on a number of occasions. Thanks for being a good friend!

Jim Stewart flew both Pete Dronkers and me at low speeds around the Big Chief cliffs in a small turbo prop plane for fly-by photography. The photos were later used for the construction of topos of some of the cliffs that were difficult to photograph from the ground. This was probably the most exhilarating part of this project!

Thanks to the following individuals who made a contribution in one way or another: Bryan Bax, Patrick Cassiday, John Fox, Andrea Jensen, Will Jones, Kendall Knowles, Jason Kuchnicki, Adrian Leasure, Greg Parrott, Brian Sweeney, Amy Teeters, Ian Veach, Todd Worsfold and Jim Zellers.

—Marek Hajek

TABLE OF CONTENTS

FOREWORD

For many years, before there were any routes at Big Chief, climbers drove up and down Hwy. 89, looked up at the rock formations and thought "I wonder?" Those were the days of granite trad climbing and strict ethics. So like everyone else I casually glanced at Big Chief on the way home from Donner Summit and deemed it choss. One day my curiosity got the better of me and with some friends we hiked up to have a look. We arrived at the south end of the cliff and stared at it for a long while. Was it loose choss or was it good? It was a little hard to tell, with no routes in sight and thick brush along the base. But after closer inspection we proclaimed the rock was worthy of routes and continued hiking along the base to get an idea of the full potential. As we explored the cliff our excitement grew. Tons of nice looking lines and not a bolt in sight. We saw lines that later became classics such as *Festus*, *Scalper* and *Pow Wow*, just waiting for a first ascent. Next, we came upon a big cave that holds the classic climb *All Guns Blazing* and knew we were onto a great find. A few days later we hiked up with bolting gear and established *War Path* and *Scalper*, the first routes put up at Big Chief. The next day we bagged *Pow Wow* and *Peace Pipe*. Steep gymnastic moves, solid rock and potential for many new routes had our crew stoked on Big Chief.

The big question was "would anybody else like it?" At first, the answer from the local community was a BIG NO. People said the rock was loose and the routes were crap. I even got a few hostile phone calls. After doing the second ascent of *Pow Wow*, Jim Zellers almost took a bad fall from the anchors because he clipped a sling that I had threaded and improperly tied in a hurry a few days before. A rumor spread quickly "Dave sabotaged the anchor and tried to kill someone." People were fuming. As a result nobody came up for at least two years. This unfortunate incident provided us time to put up routes at our leisure. The only one who competed with us for lines was Todd Worsfold.

Its been almost twenty years since the first route was put up at Big Chief. People's perception of what makes good sport climbs has changed over the years. Today, the general consensus is that Big Chief holds some of the best all around sport climbing in the Tahoe area. Big Chief offers routes spread across the ratings system that keeps a lot of climbers happy on a daily basis. The full parking lot during peak season still makes me laugh at the lack of interest from climbers during the beginning. I have put up many routes around Lake Tahoe and the Western United States. However, I feel that Big Chief has been my greatest contribution to the climbing community. Enjoy the routes!

—Dave Hatchett

PREFACE

During 2001 I began receiving e-mails from a climber that seemed obsessed with the Owens River Gorge. Almost weekly the e-mails would come rolling in, sometimes looking for beta, but most often finding miniscule errors on obscure routes that were rarely climbed. Who was this compulsive fellow?

You know the kind of guy. There are a few at every crag. They methodically attempt to climb every route at a crag. Generally starting on the easiest routes, and working through the grades, not skipping anything no matter how obscure, sparsely protected or poorly designed. They just keep climbing, guidebook in hand, marking and dating each redpoint with an unexplainable enthusiasm. If they skip a route it eats at their soul. They will ruminate for days planning to climb that route and make that mark.

Wasn't that me at one time? Faded memories swirling in my head. Wait, I've been cured, it took a lot of work, but now I'm better. I can blow off a climb and not be up all night thinking about it.

Well anyway, one day I received an e-mail from Marek inquiring about the possibility of doing a guide to his local sport crag "Big Chief". It kind of seemed like he wanted me to do it, but I was busy with other projects.

Soon he had created a table of routes with all the facts and figures necessary to do a perfect guide. Marek, being an engineer by trade, had a unique approach, obsessing on the tiniest details. All that was missing were the topos. Occasionally I would come to visit. Fantastic dinners of Spring Rolls, prepared by his wife Trang, would await. We would work into the evening, then visit Big Chief in the morning, climbing and sketching topos. I think he wanted me to draw them, but I was procrastinating, and with a bit of guidance he was soon drawing his own, some of the most technical and accurate that I've seen.

Winter came early during the fall of 2004, the gates on the road to Big Chief closed, and of course there was unfinished business. With Marek's usual zeal he hatched a plan. All we had to do was start at the bottom of the Truckee River Canyon and snowshoe up the steep slope to Little Chief, then complete an eight mile loop to every crag and formation, finishing up the remaining loose ends. It was a crisp 5°F morning, as we set out up the hillside. I tripped immediately, exploding my energy drink all over my paperwork. Later drawing a topo at Light Deprivation Buttress it must have warmed up to nearly 10°F, of course now it was snowing, frostbitten fingers scratching notes. Then back down to the river, I must have slipped and fallen a dozen times, arriving minutes before darkness. All in a days work.

Suffice to say Marek was the perfect person for the job. He has probably logged more days at Big Chief than anyone—even the Hatchett brothers; the prime developers of Big Chief. I think you will find this book to be one of the most accurate and useful guides ever. I hope you enjoy it!

—Marty Lewis

See Page 71

Greg Parrott on **Festus** 10a**** at Big Chief. ©*Jim Kovacs Photo.*

Adapted from the U.S.G.S. 1:24,000 Truckee and Tahoe City Quadrangles.

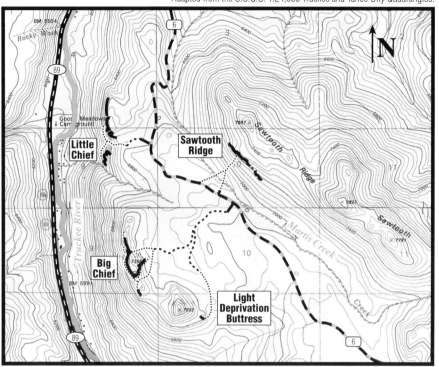

CHAPTER 1

INTRODUCTION

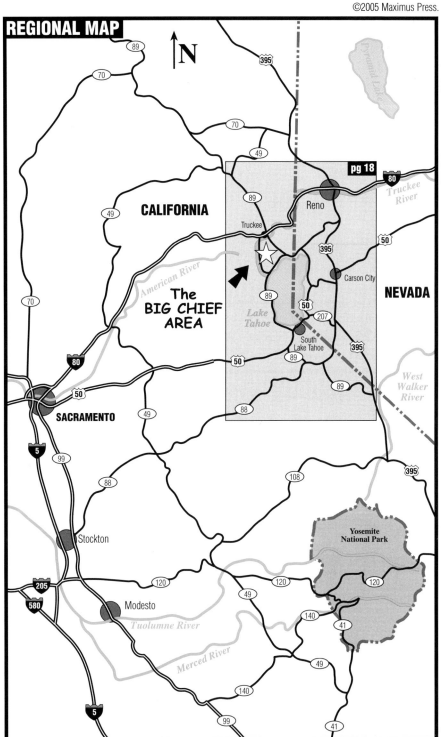

INTRODUCTION

Congratulations! You are examining the first guidebook devoted to the Big Chief Area, the location of Lake Tahoe's premier sport climbing. Over 1,500 hours of effort have been spent to bring you the most organized and accurate guide to date. I have personally climbed 111 of the 123 routes listed herein to ensure the quality and difficulty ratings are reasonable. For the latest information and route updates visit www.maximuspress.com/bigchief.

Before jumping to the climbing topos, please read the entire introduction. It is your responsibility to know the ins and outs before climbing here. Big Chief is located on public land administered by the Forest Service. Please, follow the access guidelines and try to minimize impact at this popular crag.

Big Chief is a sport climbing area. Only two routes require additional protection. The rock is composed of volcanic tuff and basalt. Routes are typically on nearly vertical or overhanging rock with positive holds. A good path along the base of the cliffs provides easy access to most of the climbs.

Comments

Some ratings have been revised based on the consensus of several climbers Quality ratings were compiled and averaged based on the feedback from climbers like you.

I would love to hear from you, so please e-mail me comments on the routes you climb, your opinion on route and quality ratings, the campgrounds you stay in, where you ran into the most bees, new route information, and anything else in connection with this guide. Your comments will help to perfect future editions of this guide. E-mail address: BigChiefGuide@hotmail.com

Where is Big Chief?

Big Chief is located in California, between the town of Truckee and Lake Tahoe. The cliffs are situated above the Truckee River Canyon on the east ridge line. Big Chief can easily be seen from Hwy. 89 about 5.3 miles south of Truckee.

Driving Times:

It takes about 25 minutes to reach the Big Chief parking areas from central Truckee, two hours from Sacramento and one hour from Reno. Weather in the mountains can be unpredictable at any time of year. Check the latest road conditions before you leave: ☎ (800) 427-7623.

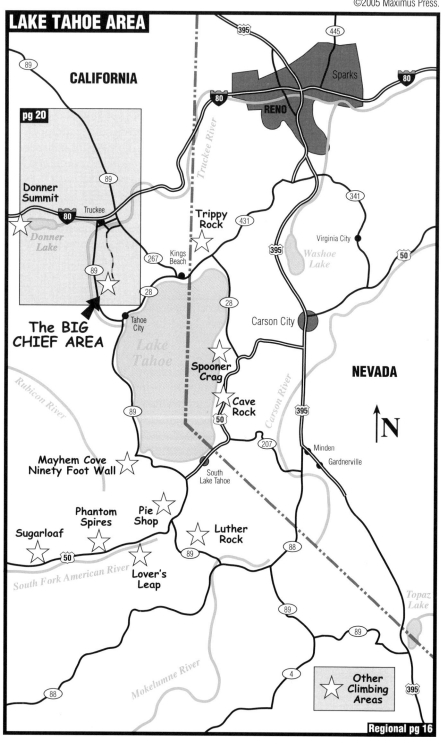

LAKE TAHOE AREA

89

CALIFORNIA

395

445

80

Sparks

RENO

80

pg 20

Donner
Summit

Truckee

80

89

Truckee River

341

89

Donner
Lake

267

Kings
Beach

**Trippy
Rock**

431

Virginia City

395

Washoe
Lake

50

89

28

The BIG
CHIEF AREA

Tahoe
City

28

Carson City

Lake
Tahoe

**Spooner
Crag**

NEVADA

Rubicon River

89

**Cave
Rock**

50

Carson River

395

207

Minden

Gardnerville

**Mayhem Cove
Ninety Foot Wall**

South
Lake Tahoe

**Phantom
Spires**

**Pie
Shop**

Sugarloaf

50

**Luther
Rock**

89

88

South Fork American River

**Lover's
Leap**

N

89

Topaz
Lake

89

Mokelumne River

4

88

395

Other
Climbing
Areas

Regional pg 16

Climate

The climbing routes at Big Chief are at an elevation of approximately 7,000 ft. The rock can be climbed the whole year round. For a full day of climbing the best climbing seasons are fall and late spring. During the summer, it is best to climb in the mornings until about 1:00 P.M. It can get quite hot in the sun in the afternoon. There are a few cliffs that are out of the sun in the afternoon. These are pointed out in the guidebook. In the fall and late spring it is cool enough to climb in the sun. On cooler days it is actually desirable to climb at Big Chief in the afternoon since it can get quite cold at this elevation in the morning. Climbing is possible in the winter on warm sunny afternoons, by parking at the 1st gate on Forest Service Route #6 and snowmobiling to the crags.

Camping

Camping is not permitted at or near Big Chief on Forest Service land. The Forest Service calls this a "restricted recreational area." Do not camp, bivouac, or park overnight at Big Chief or the Big Chief parking area. Illegal camping will cause access problems. Make the 25 minute drive to Truckee to one of the campgrounds.

Although, it is possible to camp in the woods in non-restricted recreational areas on Forest Service land, you must obtain a free camping permit beforehand from the Forest Service. The Forest Service publishes a free comprehensive camping & picnicking guide. Please, visit the Forest Service station for more information or to obtain the free camping permit at:

Truckee Ranger District
10342 Highway 89 North
Truckee, CA 96161
Phone: (530) 587-3558
TDD: (530) 587-6907
Summer Hours: (Mo-Sa) 8:00 A.M.—5:00 P.M.
Winter Hours: (Mo-Fr) 8:00 A.M.—4:30 P.M.

Fees at the campgrounds are subject to change. Please, call or visit the Forest Service for the latest fee schedule. Reservations can be made where available for Forest Service Campgrounds by calling (877) 444-6777. Reservations for the Donner Memorial State Park Campground can be made by calling (800) 444-7275.

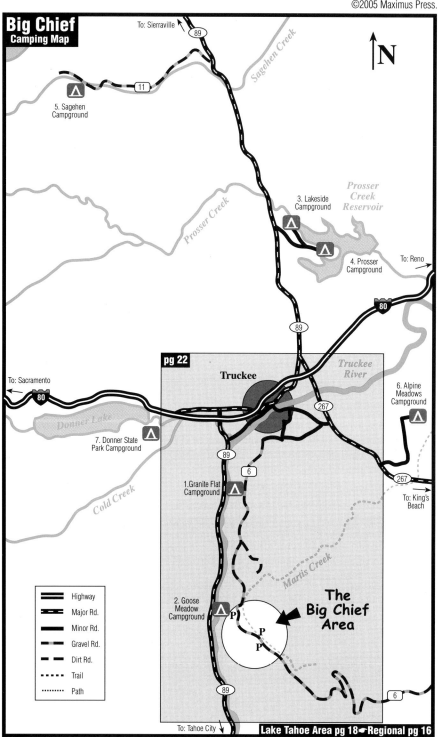

Big Chief
Camping Map

To: Sierraville 89

11

5. Sagehen
Campground

N

Sagehen Creek

Prosser Creek

Prosser
Creek
Reservoir

3. Lakeside
Campground

4. Prosser
Campground

To: Reno

80

89

pg 22

To: Sacramento

80

Truckee

Truckee
River

267

6. Alpine
Meadows
Campground

Donner Lake

7. Donner State
Park Campground

89

6

267

To: King's
Beach

1.Granite Flat
Campground

Cold Creek

Martis Creek

The
Big Chief
Area

2. Goose
Meadow
Campground

P

P
P

▬▬▬	Highway
▬▪▬	Major Rd.
▬▬▬	Minor Rd.
▬ ▬ ▬	Gravel Rd.
▬ ▬	Dirt Rd.
.....	Trail
....	Path

6

To: Tahoe City

1. Granite Flat Campground

Fee: $12/night. Additional $2 on holidays. $5 for additional vehicles. The campground host visits on site to collect fee.
Open: Year-round. No plowing in winter.
Directions: Drive 0.8 miles south of Hwy. 89/W. River St. intersection, on Hwy. 89. Campground is located on the left side.
GPS: N39.30271, W120.20548. **Elevation:** 5,856 feet.
Facilities: 75 tent or RV campsites. 7 walk-in campsites. Piped water, vault toilets.
Comments: Somewhat close to the road. Annoying road noise.
Phone: (530)587-3558. **Reservations:** (877)444-6777.

2. Goose Meadow Campground

Fee: $12/night. Additional $2 on holidays. $5 for additional vehicles. The campground host visits on site to collect fee.
Open: May through September.
Directions: Drive 4.0 miles south of Hwy. 89/W. River St. intersection, on Hwy 89. Campground is located on the left side.
GPS: N39.25926, W120.21096. **Elevation:** 5,973 feet.
Facilities: 25 campsites. Hand pump wells, vault toilets.
Comments: Somewhat close to the road. Annoying road noise but not as bad as Granite Flat Campground.
Phone: (530)587-3558. **Reservations:** (877)444-6777.

3. Lakeside Campground

Fee: $12/night. Additional $2 on holidays. $5 for additional vehicles. The campground host visits on site to collect fee.
Open: May through mid September.
Directions: Drive 3.7 miles north of Interstate 80/Hwy. 267 intersection, on Hwy. 89. Turn right and drive 1.1 miles. Campground is located on the left side.
GPS: N39.38081, W120.16898. **Elevation:** 5,747 feet.
Facilities: 30 undesignated campsites. Piped water, vault toilets, picnic tables, fire pits with grills.
Comments: Not as many trees as Prosser campground just half a mile away. Located right next to water.
Phone: (530)587-3558. **Reservations:** None.

4. Prosser Campground

Fee: $12/night. Additional $2 on holidays. $5 for additional vehicles. The campground host visits on site to collect fee.
Open: May through mid October
Directions: Drive 3.7 miles north of Interstate 80/Hwy 267 intersection, on Hwy 89. Turn right and drive 1.5 miles. Campground is located on the left side.
GPS: N39.37785, W120.16240. **Elevation:** 5,771 feet.
Facilities: 29 campsites. Piped water, vault toilets, picnic tables, fire pits with grills.
Comments: Nice campground with lots of trees. Short distance to reservoir.
Phone: (530)587-3558. **Reservations:** None.

5. Sagehen Campground

Fee: Free.
Open: While road is accessible.
Directions: Drive 8.3 miles north of Interstate 80/Hwy. 267 intersection, on Hwy. 89. Turn left before a garage on left side of road. Drive on Forest Service road #11. Once on the dirt roads, signs clearly mark directions. Last 1/4 mile of road is paved. You will encounter alternating rough and smooth sections of road. Roughest road is inside campground!
GPS: N39.43437, W120.25703. **Elevation:** 6,456 feet.
Facilities: 10 campsites. Vault toilets. No water or garbage disposal.
Comments: Nice campground with lots of trees. Low clearance vehicles need to pay attention to protruding rocks on the approach.
Phone: (530)587-3558. **Reservations:** None.

6. Alpine Meadows Campground

Fee: $10/night. Gold card: $5. Self register.
Open: April through mid October
Directions: Drive 1.4 miles southeast of Hwy. 267/Brockway Rd. intersection, on Hwy. 267 toward Lake Tahoe. Turn left at Alpine Meadows turnoff. Drive another 1.4 miles until you reach the turn off to the campground on the right side.
GPS: N39.32006, W120.12208. **Elevation:** 5,871 feet.
Facilities: 25 campsites. Pay phone, drinking water, vault toilets, fire pits with grills.
Comments: Nice campground with trees. Short distance to reservoir.
Phone: (530)587-3113. **Reservations:** None.

7. Donner State Park Campground

Fee: $15/night. 8 people per site, 1 vehicle. Additional vehicles: $4.
Open: Memorial day through mid September
Directions: Located inside Donner Memorial State Park. Drive 0.3 miles west of Interstate 80/Donner Pass Rd. intersection on Donner Pass Rd. Turn left into Donner State Park.
GPS: N39.32356, W120.23204. **Elevation:** 5,960 feet.
Facilities: 154 campsites. Drinking water, picnic tables, hot pay showers and rest rooms.
Comments: Nice campground with trees. Right next to Donner Lake.
Phone: (530)582-7894. **Reservations:** (800)444-7275.

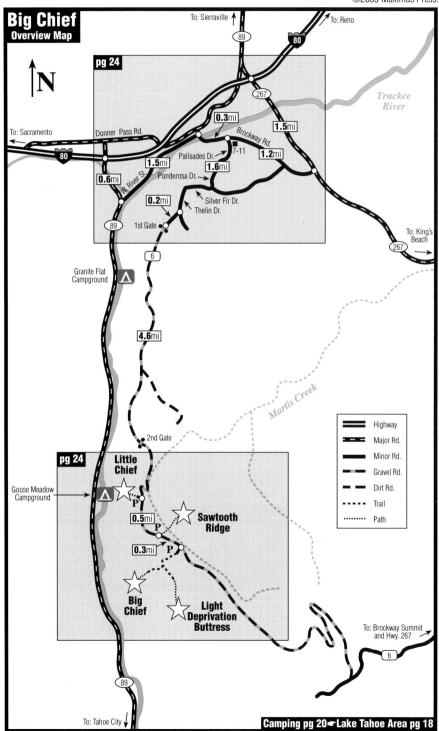

Big Chief
Overview Map

N

pg 24

To: Sierraville

To: Reno

89

80

Truckee River

0.3mi

Donner Pass Rd.

Brockway Rd.

7-11

To: Sacramento

80

0.6mi

1.5mi

Palisades Dr.

1.6mi

1.5mi

1.2mi

W. River St.

Ponderosa Dr.

0.2mi

Silver Fir Dr.

Thelin Dr.

89

1st Gate

To: King's Beach

267

6

Granite Flat Campground

4.6mi

Martis Creek

2nd Gate

pg 24

Little Chief

Goose Meadow Campground

P

0.5mi

P

Sawtooth Ridge

0.3mi

P

Big Chief

Light Deprivation Buttress

To: Brockway Summit and Hwy. 267

6

Legend

═══ Highway
═══ Major Rd.
▬▬▬ Minor Rd.
▬ ▬ Gravel Rd.
▬ ▬ Dirt Rd.
· · · · Trail
· · · · · Path

89

To: Tahoe City

Getting There

Big Chief is accessed from Forest Service route 6. There are two gates on the access road. One at the entrance and one 3.5 miles up the road. The gates block the road from first snowfall in November/December until April/May when most of the snow thaws. Check with the Forest Service, (530) 587-3558 for latest access information. Be sure to ask about both gates! Although, it is possible to approach Big Chief from the Truckee River, off Hwy. 89, it is not recommended. Private property blocks the most direct access.

A portion of the access is on a dirt road. Neither a four wheel drive nor a high clearance vehicle is required unless there is snow on the road. There is a 100 foot section of road that gets a little washed out during heavy rains at the first uphill section after the first gate. This doesn't pose a problem for most vehicles. A sign posted at the entrance warning of snow ahead can be seen through late Spring. The sign tends to stay posted long after the section of the road to Big Chief is clear. It simply refers to the section of the road past Big Chief. Please, refer to the map on opposite page for a general overview.

The directions are best broken down into three parts. First, you'll find directions from several locations to Palisades Dr., then from Palisades Dr. to the parking areas: Little Chief, Sawtooth Ridge and Big Chief. Finally, you will find hiking directions under the introduction for each crag.

To get to Palisades Dr. from:

Reno: Take Interstate 80 to Truckee, exit #188: Hwy. 267 Lake Tahoe. The exit is approximately 27.5 miles from where North McCarren crosses Interstate 80 in Reno. Turn south (left) and drive 1.5 miles. Turn right at the light onto Brockway Rd. and drive 1.2 miles to Palisades Dr. You will see a light and a 7-11 on the left. Turn left here. See remaining directions to Big Chief on the next page.

Kings Beach: In Kings Beach, at the intersection of Hwy. 267 and Hwy. 28 take Hwy. 267 north toward Truckee. Drive 10.5 miles until you come to a second traffic light. At the light, turn left onto Brockway Rd. and drive 1.2 miles to Palisades Dr. You will see a light and a 7-11 on the left. Turn left here. See remaining directions to Big Chief on the next page.

Tahoe City: Start out by taking Hwy. 89 northwest toward Truckee. From the intersection of Hwy. 28 and Hwy. 89 drive 13 miles, turn right at the light onto W. River St. Drive 1.5 miles until you come to a stop sign. Turn right onto Brockway Rd. and continue another 0.3 miles to Palisades Dr. You will see a light and a 7-11 on the right side. Turn right here. See remaining directions to Big Chief on the next page.

Sacramento: Take Interstate 80 east to Truckee. Take the Hwy. 89 exit and go south (right) 0.6 miles toward Tahoe City. Turn left at the second light onto W. River St. Drive 1.5 miles until you come to a stop sign. Turn right onto Brockway Rd. and continue another 0.3 miles to Palisades Drive. You will see a light and a 7-11 on the right side. Turn right here. See remaining directions to Big Chief on the next page.

©2005 Maximus Press.

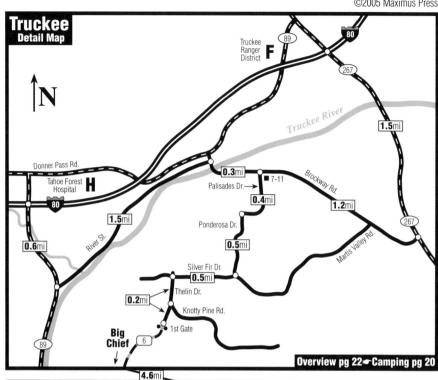

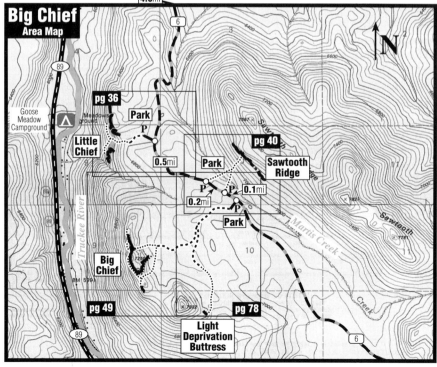

Palisades Dr. (7-11 store) to the parking areas:
Drive 0.9 miles uphill on Palisades Dr. The road is windy. Notice that Palisades Dr. becomes Ponderosa Dr. after the first 0.4 miles. Just past the crest of the hill, turn right onto Silver Fir Dr. Continue 0.5 miles and turn left onto Thelin Drive. Go 0.2 miles and turn onto a prominent forest service road on the right side. This road is paved for 0.2 miles and has a small parking area just past the gate. This is Forest Service Rd. #6. There is a sign near the entrance with the road designation. Reset your odometer at this point. You will pass another gate 3.5 miles up the road.

    IMPORTANT!!! Forest Service Rd. #6 is frequented by mountain bikers, hikers, runners, and horse riders. Please, slow down to a crawl when passing people in order not to leave them in a cloud of dust. Also, watch out for oncoming traffic.

    For Little Chief: From the first gate drive 4.6 miles on Forest Service Rd. #6. Look for a Road #6 sign on the right side just before you start heading up a steep hill. Power lines cross the road ahead. Fifty feet back is the turn off. Turn right and follow this road 400 feet downhill toward an open area where you can park. See page 37 for the approach.

    For Sawtooth Ridge: Drive 5.1 miles from the first gate on Forest Service Rd. #6. Park on the right side of Rd. #6 on an old logging road or alternately at 5.3 miles park on the left side of Rd. #6 in a clearing that looks like a plowed field. See page 41 for the approach.

    For Big Chief and Light Deprivation Buttress: At 5.4 miles past the first gate on Forest Service Rd. #6 look for a plowed-over logging road on the right side. Fifty feet past this road is another road on the right that will take you directly to the "Big Chief parking lot." Typically, there is a cairn at the entrance. Please, park responsibly so that others can find space as well. See page 48 for the Big Chief approach and page 78 for the Light Deprivation Buttress approach.

    Note: Forest Service Rd. #6 continues to Brockway Summit at the top of Hwy. 267. From the Big Chief parking lot, follow Forest Service Rd. #6 south for several miles till you reach a paved road. Turn left and stay on a paved road until you reach Brockway Summit. Total distance from Big Chief parking lot to Brockway Summit is 11.6 miles.

Approaches
There are four distinct crags in the Big Chief Area: Little Chief (8 routes), Sawtooth Ridge (15 routes), Big Chief (91 routes) and Light Deprivation Buttress (9 routes). The approach instructions are found in the introductions for each crag.

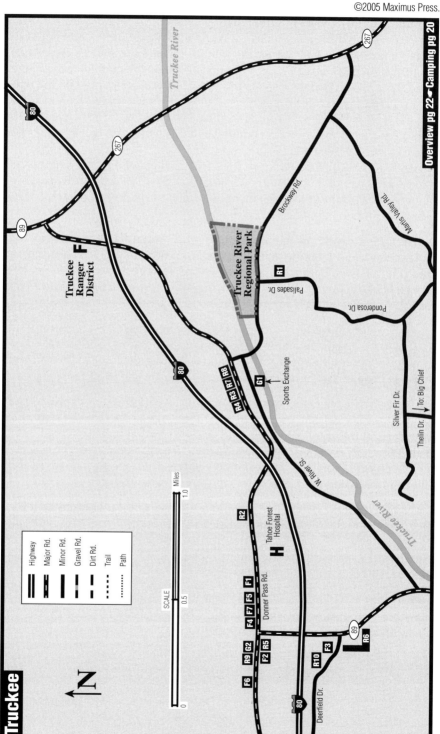

Amenities

The closest town to Big Chief is Truckee. Here, you will find an assortment of dining establishments, shops, liquor stores, and lodging. This guide highlights a few local favorites.

Fast Food

F1. Dairy Queen
11012 Donner Pass Rd.
☎ (530) 587-7055.

F2. Jalapeño Joe's
11357 Donner Pass Rd.
☎ (530) 550-7800

F3. Kentucky Fried Chicken
11412 Deerfield Dr.
☎ (530) 582-4054

F4. McDonalds
11262 Donner Pass Rd.
☎ (530) 587-3880.

F5. Port of Subs
11200-7 Donner Pass Rd.
☎ (530) 582-8060.

F6. Taco Bell
12630 Donner Pass Rd.
☎ (530) 582-4183.

F7. Round Table Pizza
11260-2 Donner Pass Rd.
☎ (530) 587-0577.

Gear/Gyms

G1. Sports Exchange
10095 West River St.
☎ (530) 582-4510
www.truckeesportsexchange.com
See advertisement on page 6.

G2. The Back Country
11400 Donner Pass Rd.
☎ (530) 582-0909

G3. RockSport Indoor Climbing Center
1901 Silverada Blvd., Reno.
☎ (775) 352-7673

Restaurants

B=Breakfast, L=Lunch, D=Dinner.

R1. Blue Coyote Bar & Grill (LD)
American food and pizza.
10015 Palisades Dr.
☎ (530) 587-7777.

R2. Café Spira (BL)
Fresh baked goods, sandwiches & hot entrées, coffee.
10770 Donner Pass Rd.
☎ (530) 550-8175.

R3. Coffee And... (BLD)
Diner.
10106 Donner Pass Rd.
☎ (530) 587-3123.

R4. El Toro Bravo (LD)
Mexican.
10186 Donner Pass Rd.
☎ (530) 587-3557.

R5. Java Sushi (D)
Sushi.
11357 Donner Pass Rd.
☎ (530) 582-1144.

R6. Los Altos (D)
Mexican.
Hwy. 89 South.
☎ (530) 587-7872.

R7. Pianeta (D)
Italian.
10098 Donner Pass Rd.
☎ (530) 587-4694.

R8. Squeeze In (BL)
10060 Commercial Row
☎ (530) 587-9814.

R9. Taco Jalisco (LD)
Mexican.
11400 Donner Pass Rd.
☎ (530) 587-1131.

R10. Wong's Garden (LD)
Chinese.
11430 Deerfield Dr.
☎ (530) 587-1831.

Access Information

There is one access issue that has existed for a number of years. In the winter, the most direct way to get to Big Chief is to hike up from the Truckee River. The most convenient bridge is on private property and the owners do not want us to cross it as is evident by the sign posted in front of the bridge "This is not access to Big Chief." I have personally spoken with the owners and this rule definitely stands. It wasn't always this way. Many years ago the owners allowed people to cross the bridge and their property, even to use their port-a-potty. Unfortunately, people have left trash and loosely scattered toilet paper behind, wrote obscene comments at the port-a-potty and ended up being rude to the owners.

You may be wondering what happened to the road between the current Big Chief parking area and the old parking area. The Forest Service "reforested" this road as part of a reforestation project. Although, not officially stated, there were some incentives for the Forest Service to do this. Climbers used to camp near the old parking lot on a regular basis—even though this area falls into a no camping zone. You guess the rest of the story...

Otherwise, there have been no access issues at Big Chief. Please, follow the simple guidelines to keep access free and the climbing areas enjoyable.

Guidelines

☞ Be respectful and courteous to Land Managers.
☞ Follow all posted rules and regulations.
☞ Never drive off of established roads.
☞ Maintain a low profile.

Environmental Concerns

Please, note that these are beautiful natural areas. Remove all signs of your passing, including tape, litter and other trash. Try to stick to established trails.

Sanitation

There are no toilets at Big Chief. If you have to relieve yourself, please hike down the slope away from the trail. Preferably take care of your business in the woods before you hike over the ridge to Big Chief. Bury waste at least six inches deep.

First Ascent Guidelines

If you are going to put up a route in the Big Chief Area, please follow these guidelines:

- ☞ Safety first. Don't put up runout routes.
- ☞ Clipping stances should be thought out thoroughly!
- ☞ Use 3/8" bolts or larger.
- ☞ In overhanging rock, use 1/2" bolts.
- ☞ No fixed pitons; use a bolt.
- ☞ On anchors use conventional hangers with "Mussy Hooks".
- ☞ Do not chip or manufacture holds.
- ☞ Gluing is acceptable to reinforce key holds, not to create holds
- ☞ Think before you drill.

Squeeze Jobs

Because of the nature of volcanic rock, just about any piece of rock can be climbed. Does this mean we should grid bolt all the formations? No! Squeeze jobs detract from the beauty of the original lines.

- ☞ If your proposed route would share numerous holds with a preexisting route it is a squeeze job.
- ☞ If a climber on your proposed route would interfere with a climber on an adjacent route it is a squeeze job.
- ☞ If bolts on your proposed route can easily be clipped from the adjacent route it is a squeeze job.

Anchors

Sling wads, chains and coldshuts are no longer appropriate anchors. After years of experimentation there is an anchor system that is quickly becoming the standard for the Big Chief Area. The anchor consists of a quick link and tow hook on a conventional bolt hanger. This system is known as a "Mussy Hook" and can be purchased from Fish Products (see advertisement on page 89) or from Maximus Press (see page 95).

Mussy Hook Anchor System.

Climbing in the Big Chief Area

Conduct

Your style of climbing is your own business. However, please operate within these simple rules:

☞ If you retreat off a route before the anchors, leave a carabiner behind. Leaving a retreat sling is ugly, dangerous, and considered bad style.

☞ Carabiners at anchors are for your convenience. Don't rip them off!

☞ Do not steal fixed ropes or quickdraws hung on routes.

☞ To help reduce wear and tear, use your own quickdraws at the anchors, especially for extended top-roping sessions. The last person on the route can take the draws down and lower or rappel from the anchor. I have seen a Boy Scout group top-rope on an anchor the whole day long. That is unacceptable here!

☞ Because of the large investment of time, energy and money involved, please don't attempt to redpoint other people's projects (these are usually marked with a red tag on the first bolt or a fixed rope).

The Rock

The rock at Big Chief is a volcanic tuff. Starting at the South Cave, heading south, including Light Deprivation Buttress, it can be abrasive to the touch on many of the routes.

Climbs at Big Chief are on nearly vertical and overhanging faces with positive holds. A number of routes have a high first bolt. If the first bolt is difficult to get to, a stick clip is recommended in the route description. The route ratings range from 5.7 to 5.13d.

Equipment

This is a sport climbing area. Only two routes require supplemental traditional gear. Most routes can be climbed with a 60m rope. A 70m rope is convenient on a few routes where two ropes are normally used to lower off. A rope bag is recommended. Over a hundred routes can be done with a rack of quickdraws. I have personally counted every bolt on every route and identified the crux to make this guidebook accurate. Keep in mind though, that people occasionally add bolts to routes and in the future my count may no longer be accurate. As a rule, take an extra couple of draws over the recommended count to avoid unpleasant surprises. Bring a means to clip off to the anchors—many of the routes require you to untie and thread the anchor.

Anchors

Most of the routes have chain anchors. Occasionally, a route will have carabiners epoxied to the chains. The majority of the routes are under 30m/100'. Routes longer than 30m/100' are marked in the book. Be safe though and always tie a knot at the end of the rope no matter how long a route is listed!

Safety Concerns

Climbing is dangerous. Always think of safety first. In case of an emergency, carry a cellular phone with you. There is cellular phone reception at Big Chief. If you are allergic to bee stings, please carry appropriate medication with you such as an epinephrine needle.

Prevention

The top three ways to get seriously injured or killed are:

#1. Climber dropped by belayer. A number of the routes in this guidebook are rope stretchers. Get in a habit of tying a knot at the end of the rope. Communicate with your belayer when getting lowered. The belayer should watch for the end of the rope.

#2. Climber failed to tie in properly. Get in the habit of checking your knot before you step off the ground and before lowering.

#3. Dropping loose rock. Holds will occasionally break, even on popular routes. Don't hang out under climbers.

Objective Hazards

I have never seen snakes at Big Chief but one can never be too cautious. Yellow jackets and wasps can be very annoying in late summer/fall. Mosquitoes are found on the approach trail in the Spring. Virtually no mosquitoes are at the climbing areas. Although rock-fall is rare, there have been accidents caused by loose rock. Wearing a climbing helmet is recommended.

In Case of an Accident

In the event of a serious injury, you should telephone for emergency help by dialing 911.

Medical care is available at:
Tahoe Forest Hospital
10121 Pine Ave
Truckee, CA 96161
☎ (530) 587-7607

To get there, drive back to Truckee. Turn left on Brockway Rd. Drive 0.4 miles and turn left on Donner Pass Rd. The Hospital is on the left after about a mile. See map page 26.

How to Use This Guide

Maps

This book features a number of exploding maps. The first is an Area Map (page 24) which shows the general layout of the Big Chief Area and the individual crags. The Area Map will help you find the individual crags and assist you in driving to them.

Approach Maps show the final parking directions as well as the hike to the crags. More complex crags may have Crag Maps and Cliff Maps. The page numbers listed with the maps will allow you to zoom in and out as necessary.

Approach Instructions

Approach instructions are found at each individual crag's introduction:

Important Note—Difficulty Ratings and Quality Ratings are not facts. These systems are subjective and based on a consensus of opinions.

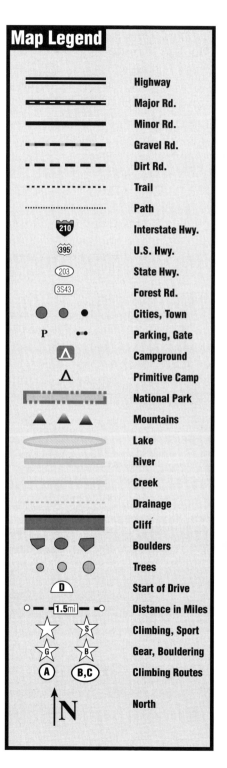

Map Legend

	Highway
	Major Rd.
	Minor Rd.
	Gravel Rd.
	Dirt Rd.
	Trail
	Path
210	Interstate Hwy.
395	U.S. Hwy.
203	State Hwy.
3S43	Forest Rd.
● ● ●	Cities, Town
P ••	Parking, Gate
△	Campground
Δ	Primitive Camp
	National Park
▲ ▲ ▲	Mountains
	Lake
	River
	Creek
	Drainage
	Cliff
▼ ● ▼	Boulders
○ ○ ○	Trees
D	Start of Drive
○━ ━1.5mi━ ━○	Distance in Miles
☆ ☆S	Climbing, Sport
☆G ☆B	Gear, Bouldering
Ⓐ B,C	Climbing Routes
↑N	North

Difficulty Ratings

Pitches have been rated according to the Yosemite Decimal System. The 5th class prefix has been dropped for simplicity. Every effort has been made to eliminate slash ratings, i.e. 10a/b. Difficulty ratings should be comparable to other sport climbing areas. More importantly, ratings are consistent amongst the routes at Big Chief.

Routes are rated for a redpoint attempt. The reason redpoint and not flash ratings were chosen is because numerous routes have tricky cruxes that take several attempts to unlock. Once you know the sequence, the rating falls into place. For example, the routes *Totally Chawsome* (12b) and *Scalper* (12b), have very technical and reachy cruxes that typically spit people off their first try. If the sequence isn't unlocked correctly these routes feel like they are in the 5.13 range.

The most difficult move does not necessarily dictate the rating of the route. For example, the hardest move on the route *Running Bull* is about 11c but the climbing is so sustained and strenuous at the crux that it warrants 11d.

Quality Ratings

Quality ratings have been assigned based on the following factors: the amount of sustained climbing, the aesthetics of the moves, pump factor, exposure, location and rock quality. Squeeze jobs, contrived lines, and poorly equipped routes subtract from the quality rating.

★★★★★	Big Chief Area Classic
★★★★	Awesome
★★★	Great
★★	Good
★	Mediocre
•	Poor

An (R, 10c) following the rating indicates a 10c move in a runout section.

Route Descriptions

Following the name and route rating is a description of the gear that is required. First, is the number of bolts, if any, followed by any gear that may be required, if any. Next is a brief description of the route. Pitches longer than 30 meters/100 feet, and then the descent information are noted. Finally listed is the first ascent information (if known). The first climber listed completed the first redpoint of each route. Subsequent climbers contributed to the route in some fashion.

Route Names

Many new routes have been added in recent years. Although much effort has been made to find the route's first ascentionist and get the route names, numerous routes remained unnamed. I have taken the liberty to name these routes until the first ascentionist lets me know what his/her route should be called.

Adapted from the U.S.G.S. 1:24,000 Truckee and Tahoe City Quadrangles.

Sawtooth Ridge. ©*Pete Dronkers Photo.*

CHAPTER 2

OUTLYING CRAGS

Adapted from the U.S.G.S. 1:24,000 Truckee Quadrangle.

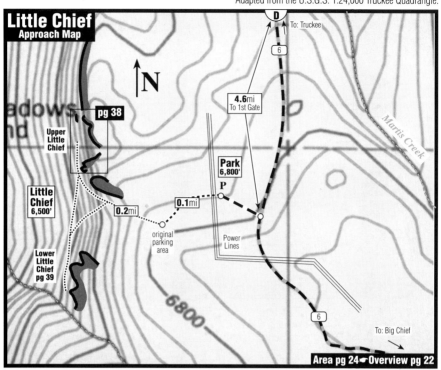

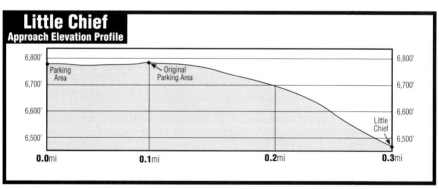

Little Chief

This little known crag contains 8 sport climbs. There is no established trail. As a result the approach, although short, is rather unpleasant. The routes don't get much traffic and tend to be gritty. This is definitely not the best climbing in the Big Chief Area. However, if you would like to

Little Chief Details
Elevation: 6,500 ft. **Exposure:** West facing, afternoon sun. **Sport Climbs:** 8 routes, 10b to 12a. **Approach:** 15 minute sandy scramble with a 300 ft. descent.

get away from the crowds, Little Chief is a good bet. The crag is west facing and gets sun in the afternoon. There are a number of large trees near the crag, offering pleasant shade.

The Approach: See *Getting There* page 23. From the first gate drive 4.6 miles on Forest Service Rd. #6. Look for a Road #6 sign on the right side just before you start heading up a steep hill. Power lines cross the road ahead. Fifty feet back is the turn off. Turn right and follow this road 400 feet downhill toward an open area where you can park.

From the parking area walk along a road for a couple hundred feet to the original parking area. Both the road and the parking area have been "reforested"—made inaccessible to vehicles through plowing. Hike directly west from the old parking area. Soon you'll be heading down a steep, sandy hill. A band of cliffs lies on the right. At the bottom of the rock formations you have a choice to turn right toward Upper Little Chief or left across a sandy slope toward Lower Little Chief.

©2005. *Marek Hajek Photo.*

©2005 Maximus Press.

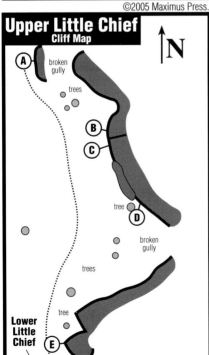

Upper Little Chief
Intro: Page 37.

A. Bong Drinker 11b*
7 bolts, crux at 2nd. Start up stemming between two mini dihedrals or just go up left dihedral. Thin sharp edges. Lower off.
FA: Dave Hatchett, Jeff McKitterick.

B. Pickled Pigs Feet 10c**
7 bolts, crux at 2nd. Two hard to reach jugs followed by a thin move through crux. Lower off.
FA: Dave Hatchett, Jeff McKitterick.

C. Tastes Like Chicken 11c***(R, 9)
5 bolts, crux 4th to 5th. 5.9 runout to first bolt. Then reachy moves between jugs. Lower off.
FA: Dave Hatchett, Mike Hatchett.

D. Shit List 12a**
4 bolts. Starts 30' right of *Tastes Like Chicken*, behind a tree. Steep face. Lower off.
FA: Dave Hatchett, Mike Hatchett.

E. Lemmiwinks 10b*
4 bolts, crux 3rd to 4th. Start on face then climb around arete. Crumbly, lichen covered rock. Lower off.
FA: Dave Hatchett, Mike Hatchett.

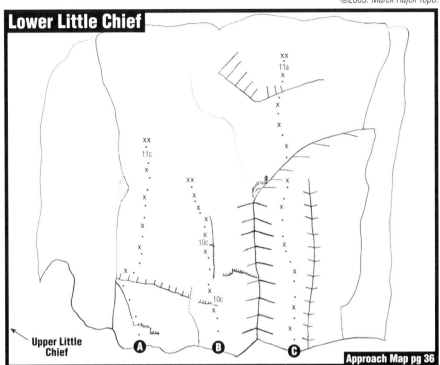

Lower Little Chief

Intro: Page 37. The sun hits around 1 P.M. This crag is well shaded by trees.

A. Foregone Conclusion 11c*
Stick clip, 5 bolts, crux 5th to anchor. Roof to slabby, ever more thinning face. Lower off.

B. Geranium 10c**
7 bolts, crux at 1st through 3rd. Dihedral to face. Lower off.

C. Beer Goggles 11a**
10 bolts, crux at 10th. Nice incut edges to a slabby bulge, then jugs through roof. Mossy. This will be an excellent route when it is cleaned up. Lower off.
FA: Dave Hatchett, Jeff McKitterick.

Adapted from the U.S.G.S. 1:24,000 Truckee and Tahoe City Quadrangles.

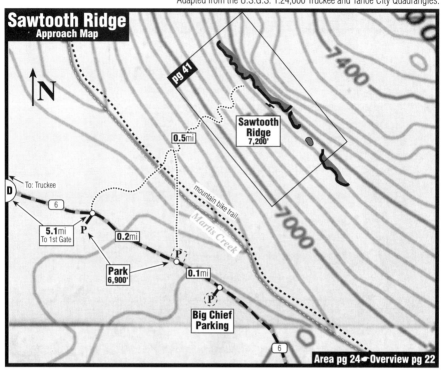

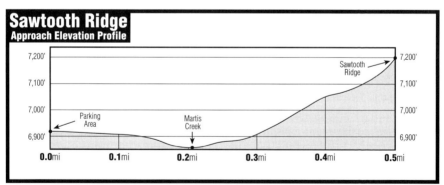

Sawtooth Ridge

Although close to Big Chief, climbing at Sawtooth Ridge is a bit more adventurous in its routes and setting. This crag gets sun around 10 in the morning, but many pines offer shady hideaways from the sun and the heat of summer. Hot afternoons should be avoided as the routes get sun all day. The climbing is generally on vertical

Sawtooth Ridge Details

Elevation: 7,200 ft.
Exposure: Southwest facing, late morning sun.
Sport Climbs: 15 routes, 5.7 to 12a.
Approach: 20 minute hike with a 300 ft. gain.

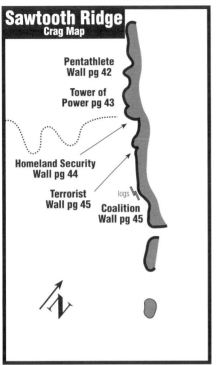

Sawtooth Ridge
Crag Map

Pentathlete
Wall pg 42

Tower of
Power pg 43

Homeland Security
Wall pg 44

Terrorist
Wall pg 45   logs   Coalition
Wall pg 45

N

Sawtooth Ridge

Pentathlete Wall

Tower of Power

Homeland Security Wall

Terrorist Wall

Coalition Wall

or slightly less than vertical rock, with holds that tend to be edgy and sharp. Two good days here will leave your skin feeling like you've been bouldering at the Buttermilks. The largest concentration of developed routes is towards the northern most end of the crag. The routes tend to be long, so bring a 60m rope and a dozen draws. A nice mix of moderate routes at Pentathlete Wall provides for good warm-ups. Sawtooth Ridge is rather new in its development and loose rock still exists on many of the routes, your belayer should remain attentive.

The Approach: See *Getting There* page 23. Drive 5.1 miles from the first gate on Forest Service Rd. #6. Park on the right side of Rd. #6 on an old logging road or alternately at 5.3 miles park on the left side of Rd. #6 in a clearing that looks like a plowed field.

From either lot hike east until you get to a streambed. Just across the streambed is a single-track mountain bike trail; from there you should be able to see the crag clearly. Hike along the single-track either north or south depending on the parking lot you've used until you find the climbers trail marked with a cairn. If the climber trail eludes you, hike the strenuous hill towards the left most visible side of the left most escarpment. On your way down, the trailhead is easily found near the large pine tree and small cave of the Homeland Security Wall. The brush looks intimidating from below but as you get into it you'll always find an easy path through it.

©2005. *Chris Kurrle Topo.*

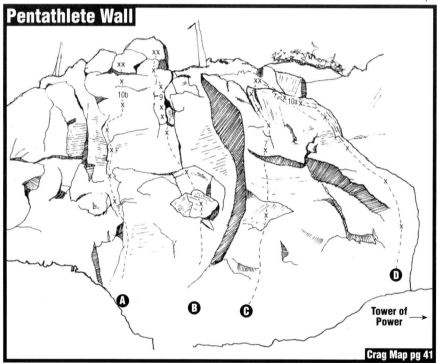

Pentathlete Wall

Crag Map pg 41

Pentathlete Wall
Sawtooth Ridge Intro: Page 40.

A. Skimmy 10b****
6 bolts, crux 5th to 6th. Climb double arête and transition to face. Crux is sequential and committing for the grade. Lower off.
FA: Chris Kurrle, Mike McCabe, 8/2004.

B. Jimmy 9**
7 bolts, crux 5th to 6th. Climb large blocks to a small chimney. Wrestle your way up the chimney to a fun face above. Lower off.
FA: Chris Kurrle, Mike McCabe, 8/2004.

C. Hunchy Bunchy Banana Pants 7***
5 bolts, crux 2nd to 3rd. Tricky start to short slab. Clip 2nd bolt and climb a small roof crux, to parallel cracks above. Climb finishes on a large ledge. Shares lower off with *Pollo del Fuego*.
FA: Chris Kurrle, Mike McCabe, 8/2004.

D. Pollo Del Fuego 10a****
6 bolts, crux 5th to 6th. Start just left of the arête, climbing the slab just right of the bolt line. Continue over the bulge to the face above. Shares lower off with *Hunchy Bunchy Banana Pants*.
FA: Chris Kurrle, Mike McCabe, 8/2004.

Tower of Power

Sawtooth Ridge Intro: Page 40.

A. Lord Braggart 12a*****

8 bolts, crux bulge at 4th and 5th to 7th. Climb interesting moves to the right of a small water streak. Pull powerful moves to mount bulge above bolt 4. REST! Bouldery moves with technical footwork lead to jugs above. Lower off.
FA: Chris Kurrle, Mike McCabe, 10/2004.

B. Project

C. Rumsfeld's Revenge 11c****

9 bolts, crux 8th to 9th. Start left of a large pine tree. Climb an easy face through a challenging roof. Very technical crux. Lower off.

©2005. *Chris Kurrle Topo.*

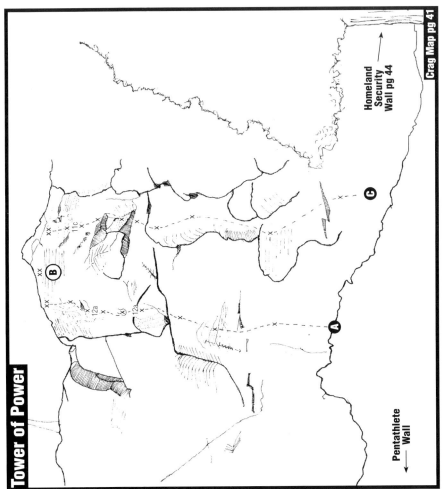

Tower of Power

Crag Map pg 41

Homeland Security Wall pg 44

Pentathlete Wall

©2005. *Chris Kurrle Topo.*

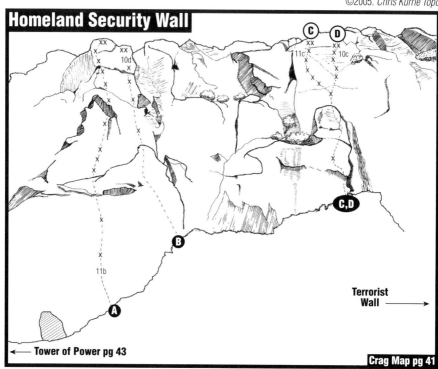

Homeland Security Wall

Terrorist Wall ⟶

◄— **Tower of Power pg 43**

Crag Map pg 41

Homeland Security Wall
Sawtooth Ridge Intro: Page 40.

A. Axis of Evil 11b****
11 bolts, crux getting to 1st. Climb crimpy face to sustained climbing on a blunt arete. Lower off.
FA: Chris Kurrle, Mike McCabe, 9/2003.

B. Threat Level Orange 10d*****
4 bolts, crux 4th to anchor. Scramble up 5.4 ledges to first bolt. Climb tricky face to a horizontal crack with a good rest. Powerful crimps and a tiny two finger pocket lead you past the crux. Lower off.
FA: Chris Kurrle, Mike McCabe, Louise Wu, 6/2004.

C. Exit Strategy 11c****
7 bolts, gear, crux 6th to 7th. Start left of an obvious water chute, sharing first 2 bolts with *Pre-emptive Strike*. Runout between bolts 1 and 2 should be protected with a medium to large cam (5.8 climbing). Climb left from bolt 2 to the base of a black streak. Crimpy sustained moves lead to the bulge "exit". Prepare your exit strategy. Lower off.
FA: Chris Kurrle, Mike McCabe, Louise Wu, 6/2004.

D. Pre-emptive Strike 10c****
6 bolts, gear, crux 6th to anchors. Start left of obvious water chute. Runout between bolts 1 and 2 should be protected with a medium to large cam (5.8 climbing). Sustained thin slab with awesome edging to anchors. Lower off.

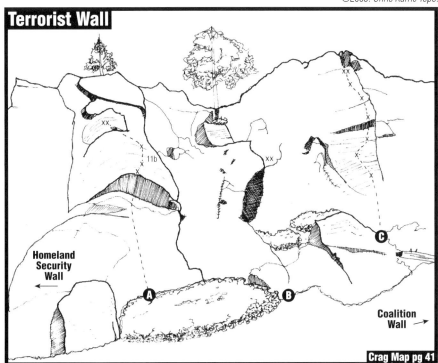

Terrorist Wall
Sawtooth Ridge Intro: Page 40.

A. R.P.G. 11b***
3 bolts, crux 2nd to 3rd. Short climb with fun bouldery moves. Lower off.

B. Spider Hole ?
Bolts. Starts inside a small cave, climbing past several bolts. End just outside cave. Lower off.

C. Shock & Awe ?
6 bolts. Climb past 3 bolts to small roof. 3 more bolts lead to the anchors. Lower off.

Coalition Wall
D. Sixteen Virgins 10d****
Stick clip, 10 bolts, crux to 1st and 8th to 9th. The route begins right of large fallen trees, behind a pine tree. Start on sharp edges then diverse face, dihedral, lieback and thin face. Great moderate climbing between cruxes. Lower off.
FA: Dave Hatchett.

E. Weapons of Mass Destruction 12a***
9 bolts, crux 1st to 2nd (11c) and 9th to the anchors. Climb a loose water streak over a bulge. Moderate climbing leads to a powerful, committing crux with desperate blind tosses. Lower off.
FA: Chris Kurrle, Mike McCabe, 9/2003.

See Page 55

Dave Hatchett on **Medicine Man** 12a** at the Oven. ©*Mike Hatchett Photo.*

Adapted from the U.S.G.S. 1:24,000 Truckee and Tahoe City Quadrangles.

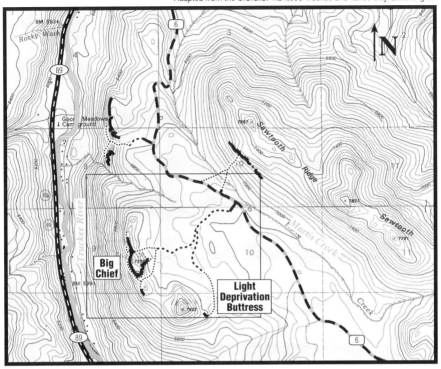

CHAPTER 3

BIG CHIEF AREA

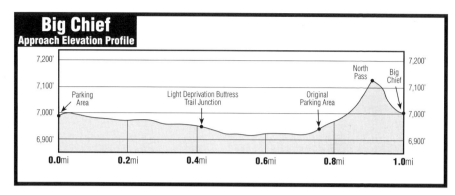

Big Chief
Approach Elevation Profile

Parking Area — Light Deprivation Buttress Trail Junction — Original Parking Area — North Pass — Big Chief

7,200' · 7,100' · 7,000' · 6,900'

0.0mi   0.2mi   0.4mi   0.6mi   0.8mi   1.0mi

Big Chief

The Approach: See *Getting There* page 23. At 5.4 miles past the first gate on Forest Service Rd. #6 look for a plowed-over logging road on the right side. Fifty feet past this road is another road on the right that will take you directly to the "Big Chief parking lot." Typically, there is a cairn at the entrance. Please, park responsibly so that others can find space as well.

Big Chief Details

Elevation: 7,000 ft.
Exposure: Varied, mostly west facing, afternoon sun.
Sport Climbs: 91 routes, 5.8 to 13d.
Approach: 30 minute hike with a 200 ft. gain and descent.

From the parking lot, follow a logging road southwest for about 0.8 miles. In the spring and early summer, you will pass a large puddle formed in the ruts of the old logging road. The puddle can be safely avoided on either side. The logging road ends at the old parking lot. From this parking lot follow a prominent trail heading west and straight uphill toward the crest of the ridge

Big Chief Parking
Point of View

To: Forest Rd. 6

Adapted from the U.S.G.S. 1:24,000 Tahoe City and Truckee Quadrangles.

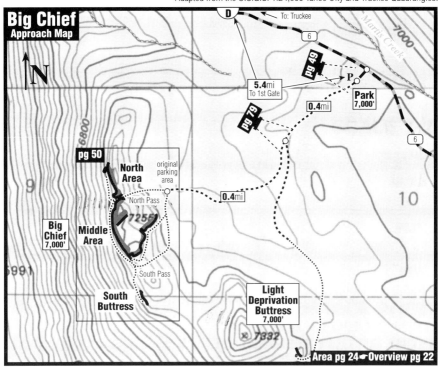

for about 500 feet. Crest the ridge and follow the trail downhill. After about 50 feet you will have the choice to head toward the North Area on the right or the Middle Area on the left.

There is another way to approach the Middle and South Areas. At the end of the logging road, just before you enter the old parking lot, there is a trail

©2005. *Marek Hajek Photo.*

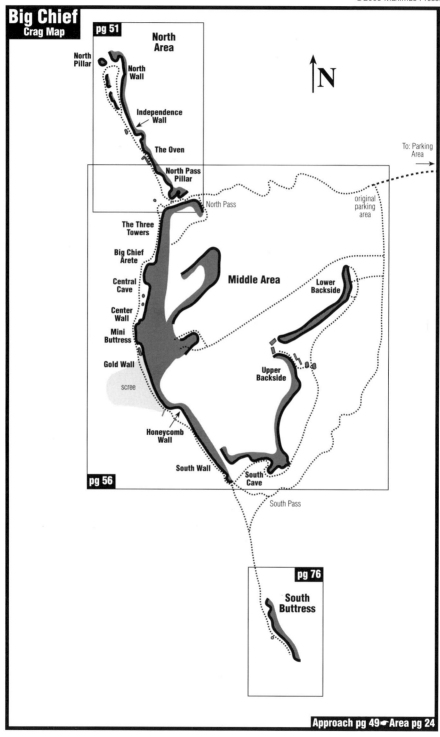

Big Chief
Crag Map

pg 51

North Area

North Pillar

North Wall

Independence Wall

The Oven

North Pass Pillar

North Pass

The Three Towers

Big Chief Arete

Central Cave

Center Wall

Mini Buttress

Gold Wall

scree

Honeycomb Wall

South Wall

South Cave

Middle Area

Lower Backside

Upper Backside

original parking area

To: Parking Area

N

South Pass

pg 56

pg 76

South Buttress

Approach pg 49 ☞ Area pg 24

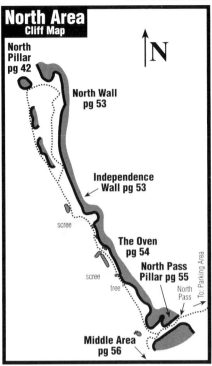

North Area
Cliff Map

N

North
Pillar
pg 42

North Wall
pg 53

Independence
Wall pg 53

scree

The Oven
pg 54

North Pass
Pillar pg 55

scree

tree

North
Pass

To: Parking Area

Middle Area
pg 56

North Area

North
Pillar

North
Wall

Independence Wall

The Oven

North Pass
Pillar

North Pass

that goes left (south). Follow this trail at a gentle uphill. You will pass the backside routes of Big Chief which are best climbed in the late afternoon during the hot summer months. After about 500 feet, the trail heads up a steep hill. Once you crest the ridge, you will find yourself at the South Pass. Follow a trail down and toward the right to approach the Middle Area. Optionally, head left after about 100 feet downhill to reach the South Buttress climbing area.

©2005. *Marek Hajek Photo.*

©2005. *Marty Lewis Topo.*

©2005. *Marek Hajek Topo.*

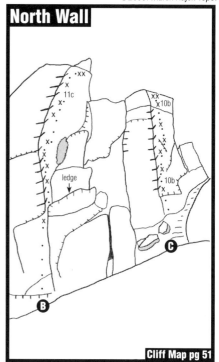

North Pillar

Big Chief Intro: Page 48. Located 500 feet north of the Oven. From the Oven, follow a trail over a short loose section of scree followed by a path through brush. Take the lower trail at a fork about 350 feet north of the Oven to get to the North Pillar. Some bushwhacking required. In the summer this crag comes into the sun around noon.

A. North Pillar 10a**

3 bolts, crux 2nd to 3rd. Detached pillar. Face to fragmented seam. Abrasive rock. Lower off.
FA: Dave Hatchett, Jeff McKitterick, 1994.

©2005. *Marek Hajek Photo.*

Independence Wall

Cliff Map pg 51

North Wall

Big Chief Intro: Page 48. Located 500 feet north of the Oven. From the Oven, follow a trail over a short loose section of scree followed by a path through brush. Take the uphill trail at a fork about 350 feet north of the Oven to get to the North Wall. In the summer this crag comes into the sun around noon.

B. High Tide 11c**
8 bolts, crux 7th to 8th. Eroded looking face to fragmented overhanging crack. Abrasive rock. Lower off.
FA: Joe Missick, 1994.

C. Laas Rocket 10b*
6 bolts, crux 1st to 2nd and 6th to anchor. Jagged holds and flakes on vertical face. Dirty, abrasive rock. Lower off.
FA: Dave Hatchett, Phil Kettner, 1994.

Independence Wall

Big Chief Intro: Page 48. Located about 200 feet north of the oven. Follow a trail over a short loose section of scree. After another 75 feet bushwhack to a fourth class right leaning ramp. Climb this ramp to a wide ledge. In the summer this crag comes into the sun around 12:30 P.M.

D. Jeronimo 12b*
7 bolts, crux 3rd to 4th. Small pockets and edges on overhanging wall to lichen covered face. Rotten rock. Lower off.
FA: Joe Missick, Mike Eadington, 1994.

E. Jeronimo Drinking Fire Water 12c·
6 bolts, crux 3rd to anchor. Small pockets and edges on overhanging wall to a bulge. Loose and rotten rock. Climb up first 4 bolts on *Jeronimo*, then traverse right. Lower off.
FA: Joe Missick, Mike Eadington, 1994.

F. Firewater 12d·
6 bolts, crux 3rd to 4th. Small pockets and edges on overhanging wall to a bulge. Loose and rotten rock. Climb up first 3 bolts on *Jeronimo*, then traverse right. Lower off.
FA: Joe Missick, Mike Eadington, 1994.

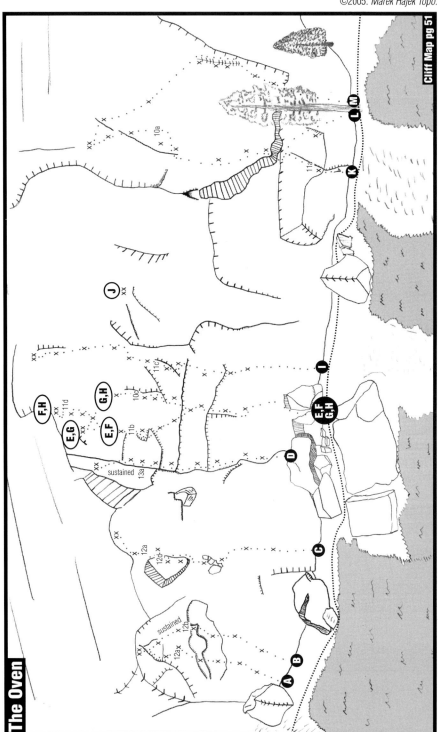

The Oven

Cliff Map pg 51

©2005. Marek Hajek Topo.

North Pass Pillar

Cliff Map pg 51

The Oven

Big Chief Intro: Page 48. Located about 350 feet north of the North Pass. Follow a trail to a prominent concave area. In the summer this crag comes into the sun by 12:30 P.M.

A. Medicine Man 12a**
6 bolts, crux 5th to 6th. Blocky, overhanging face. Sharp, edgy pieces of rock characterize holds. Tough on the fingers. Lower off. ➤ Photo page 46.
FA: Dave Hatchett, Mike Hatchett, 1993.

B. Freak of Nature 12b**
6 bolts, crux 4th to anchor. Blocky, overhanging face. Sustained from 4th bolt on. A bit contrived. Sharp, edgy pieces of rock characterize holds. Tough on the fingers. Lower off.
FA: Jim Surette, Dave Hatchett, 1993.

C. Climb Against Nature 12d***
8 bolts crux 6th to 8th. Face to overhanging crack. Then past a bulge on steeply overhanging wall. Lower off.
FA: Dave Hatchett, Dave Griffith, 1992.

D. Crackle 13a·
8 bolts, crux 6th to 8th. Blocky face to crack in middle of steeply overhanging wall. Very sharp rock crystals inside crack. Lower off.
FA: John Fox. Bolts: Erick Walker.

E. Undercooked 11b****
8 bolts, crux 7th to 8th. Head left at the 4th bolt up overhanging face. Short people tend to dyno through crux. Lower off.
FA: Dave Hatchett, Mike Hatchett, 1993.

F. Overcooked 11d**
11 bolts, crux 11th to anchor. Extension to *Undercooked*. Climb *Undercooked*, then climb right of the anchor up overhanging face. Lower off.
FA: Dave Hatchett, Mike Hatchett, 1993.

G. Halfbaked 10c***
9 bolts, crux at 7th. Great jugs up overhanging face. Head right at 4th bolt into a dihedral system. Lower off.
FA: Dave Hatchett, Mike Hatchett, 1993.

H. Superbaked 11d**
11 bolts, crux 11th to anchor. Extension to *Halfbaked*. Climb *Halfbaked*, then right of the anchor up overhanging face. Lower off.
FA: Dave Hatchett, Mike Hatchett, 1993.

I. Bun in the Oven 11c***
10 bolts, crux 5th to 6th. Climb up blocky face. Reachy crux along right leaning ramp. Lower off.
FA: Dave Hatchett, Mike Hatchett, 1993.

J. Open Project ?
This is an abandoned route. Feel free to finish it.

K. Sundance Variation 11a**
8 bolts, crux at 1st. Direct, bouldery start to *Sundance*. Lower off.
FA: Dean Barbis, 1994.

L. Sundance 10a***
8 bolts, crux at 6th. Climb to the top of a block, then a mix between fragmented crack and face climbing. Lower off.
FA: Dean Barbis, 1994.

M. Sunshine 10b***
7 bolts. Climb over and around several bulges to thin slabby face. Sustained climbing. Lower off.

North Pass Pillar

N. Travail Buttress 10d***(R, 7)
4 bolts, crux 3rd to 4th, runout on 5.7 ground or optional gear to 3.5'. Easy climbing along a crack system to a ledge. Then tackle a steep face with small slabby holds and an occasional finger slot. A bit sporty at the crux. Lower off.
FA: Todd Worsfold, Kathy Bennet, 6/1990.

O. Open Project ?
This is an abandoned project. Feel free to finish it.
P: Dave Hatchett.

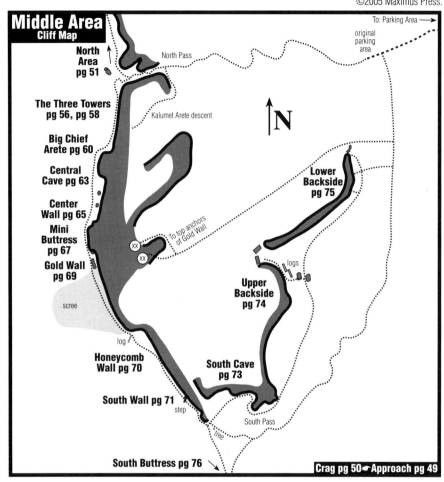

Middle Area
Cliff Map

To: Parking Area →

original parking area

North Area pg 51

North Pass

The Three Towers pg 56, pg 58

Kalumet Arete descent

Big Chief Arete pg 60

Central Cave pg 63

Center Wall pg 65

Mini Buttress pg 67

To top anchors of Gold Wall

XX

XX

Lower Backside pg 75

N

Gold Wall pg 69

scree

logs

Upper Backside pg 74

log

log

Honeycomb Wall pg 70

South Cave pg 73

South Wall pg 71

step

South Pass

tree

South Buttress pg 76

Crag pg 50 ← Approach pg 49

The Three Towers - Left Wall

Big Chief Intro: Page 48. First climbing area south of the North pass. In the summer this crag comes into the sun around 1:30 P.M.

A. Eye of the Beholder 11d***
Stick clip, 5 bolts, crux 4th to 5th. Fragmented crack to overhanging head wall. Lower off.
FA: Rick Lovelace, Dave Hatchett, 6/1990.

B. Headband 11c***
Stick clip, 4 bolts, crux 2nd to 3rd. Very technical steep face to small roof. Sustained hard climbing. Lower off.
FA: Dave Hatchett, Rick Lovelace, 6/1990.

C. Sitting Bull 11c**
Stick clip, 3 bolts, crux 2nd to 3rd. Climb to a horn, then a bouldery move over a small roof leads to easier climbing. Lower off.
FA: Dave Hatchett, Rick Lovelace, 6/1990.

D. Flame Thrower 10d****
15 bolts, crux 2nd to 3rd. Start in a mini-dihedral follow with a mix of face climbing to a crack finish. 36m route, you can lower with a 70m rope very carefully! Otherwise use two ropes to get off.
FA: Dave Hatchett, Jeff McKitterick, 1992.

E. Running Bull 11d***
12 bolts, crux 9th to 12th. 25m/85' of difficult climbing leads to a long, strenuous, thin section. 37m route, you can lower with a 70m rope very, very carefully! Otherwise use two ropes to get off! ☞ The author of this climb purposely took whippers at the crux on lead to ensure the falls are safe.
FA: Todd Worsfold.

F. Livestock Pasture 10a·
See following page.

©2005. *Marek Hajek Topo.*

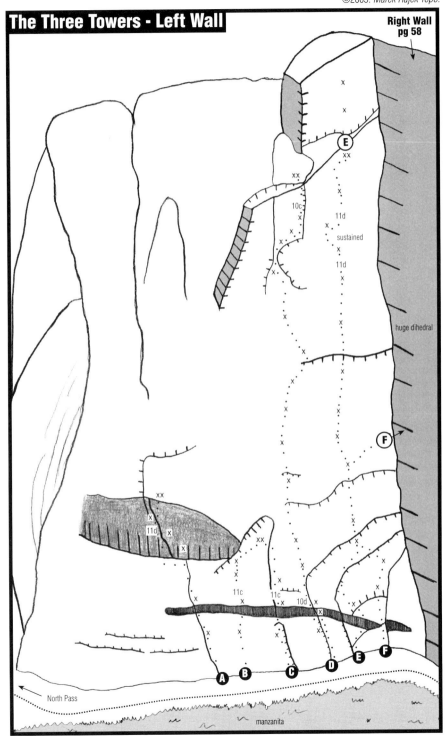

The Three Towers - Right Wall

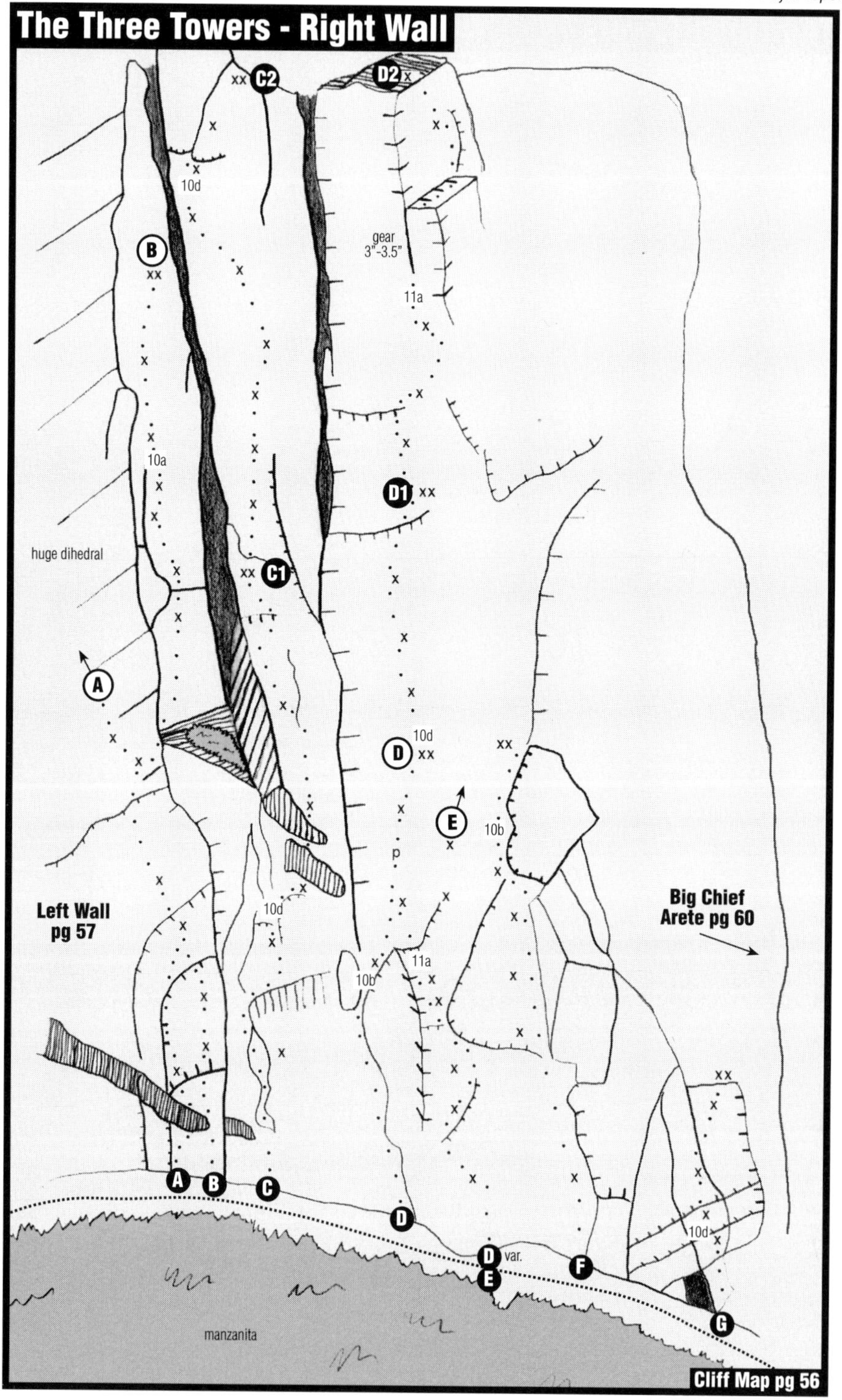

C2
D2
10d
gear 3"-3.5"
B
11a
10a
D1
huge dihedral
C1
A
10d
D
E
10b
10d
Left Wall pg 57
Big Chief Arete pg 60
11a
10b
10d
A
B
C
D
D var.
E
F
G
manzanita
Cliff Map pg 56

The Three Towers - Right Wall
Big Chief Intro: Page 48.

A. Running Bull 11d***
See previous page.

B. Livestock Pasture 10a·
11 bolts, crux 9th to 10th. Start up a vegetated wide crack to a dirty and loose gully. Then up a face on a lichen covered column. Bolts 3-5 are shared with *Running Bull*. Use a long sling on bolt #5. 36m route, you can lower with a 70m rope very carefully! Rope has a tendency to get stuck in gully when pulled.

C. Green Hornet 10d*(R, 10a)
Pitch 1: 10d*(R, 10a). Stick clip, 5 bolts crux 2nd to 3rd. Crack system to a gritty face. Belay at first anchor on comfortable stance. Too much rope drag to do as one pitch. Climb 2nd pitch or lower off.
FA: Todd Worsfold.

Pitch 2: 10d*. 8 bolts crux 6th to 7th. Lichen covered face with sharp edges and sidepulls to a diagonal crack. A bit loose & crumbly. Lower off to midway anchors.
FA: Todd Worsfold.

D. Kalumet Arete 11a**
Pitch 1: 10d*. 6 bolts, 1 piton, gear to 3.5", long slings. Original trad line. Start a dihedral system then climb up a face past an anchor (optionally stop here for a 10b pitch) and continue past 3 more bolts. Climb 2nd pitch or 30m/100' lower off.
FA: Todd Worsfold, Dick Richardson, 5/1990.

Pitch 1 sport variation: 11a***. 11 bolts and a piton, crux 5th to 6th. Preferred sport climber's variation. Climb a sequence of face, undercling, technical crux and more face climbing. 30m/100' to 2nd anchor. Clean draws while lowering to make it down safely.

Pitch 2: 11a*. 4 bolts, gear to 3.5". This pitch is a bit loose. Anchors are inconvenient to belay from. Bring gear to 2.5" to reinforce anchor. Best to walk off the top.
FA: Todd Worsfold, Dick Richardson, 5/1990.

E. Project
F. Lost Souls 10b**
5 bolts, crux 5th to anchor. Climb a lichen covered face to an undercling heading left to an interesting chimney section. Lower off.

G. Thrash Under Pressure 10d**
Stick clip, 4 bolts, crux 2nd. Climb a short, blocky, overhanging face by hugging the blocks on both sides. Lower off.
FA: Mike Hatchett, Dave Hatchett, Jeff McKitterick, 1993.

See Page 63

The late Bill Bradshaw on **All Guns Blazing** 13a****. ©*Bryan Bax Photo.*

©2005. *Marek Hajek Photo.*

Big Chief Arete

11a

11a

10c

10c

The Three
Towers pg 59

Central
Cave pg 63

Cliff Map pg 56

Big Chief Arete

Intro: Page 48. South of the North pass. In the summer this crag comes into the sun by 1 P.M.

A. Head Rush 11a***

12 bolts, crux at 10th. Start behind a small evergreen tree. The climb begins as a face climb on small edges. A nice rest in the middle awaits before more difficult, steep climbing. The person lowered off has the tendency to end up downhill to the right of the belayer. Be careful with a 60m rope! 30m/100' lower off.
FA: Dave Hatchett, Jeff McKitterick, 1993.

B. Funambulist 10c**

8 bolts. The route starts up a slabby ramp, then climb over several blocks before reaching a slabby finish. Use long slings to avoid rope drag. Lower off.

C. Big Chief Arete 11a***

15 bolts, crux 12th to 13th. Begin by stemming through a dihedral system for 30'. Then tackle blocky face, climb past the anchor of *Funambulist* over a bulge to a gritty finish. Long slings on lower bolts will lessen rope drag. 40m/130' double rope rappel.
FA: Dave Hatchett, Jeff McKitterick, 1992.

Variation: 10c***. 10 bolts, crux 3rd to 4th and at 8th. Stop at the anchor of *Funambulist*. Lower off.

See Page 63

Dave Hatchett on **Totally Chawsome** 12b****. ©*Mike Hatchett Photo.*

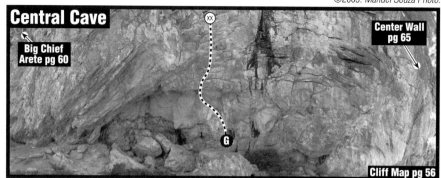

©2005. *Manuel Souza Photo.*

Central Cave

Big Chief Arete pg 60

Center Wall pg 65

Cliff Map pg 56

Marek Hajek gettin' **Totally Chawsome** 12b****. ©*Jim Kovacs Photo.*

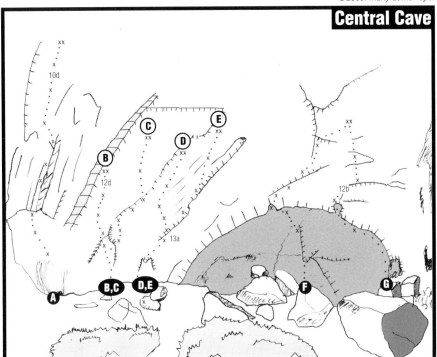

Central Cave

Central Cave
Big Chief Intro: Page 48.

A. Killer Bee 10d★★★
9 bolts, crux 8th to 9th. Climb a blocky section, around corner and up an overhanging bulge. Lower off.
FA: Dave Hatchett, Jeff McKitterick, 1992.

B. Wicked Quickie 12d★★★
4 bolts, crux 4th to anchor. Short, powerful, bouldery route. Original ascent goes a couple moves past the anchor. Lower off.
FA: Dave Hatchett, Mike Hatchett, 1992.

C. Vulgar Display of Power 13c★★
Stick clip, 6 bolts. Start up a bolt line that parallels *Wicked Quickie* then head right, up overhanging face. Lower off.
FA: Dave Hatchett, Mike Hatchett, 1992.

D. Blazing Buckets 13b★★★
Stick clip, 5 bolts. Climb to the 2nd bolt on *All Guns Blazing*, then go straight out the roof. Some holds broke off. May be harder now. ➤ Front cover photo.
FA: Dave Hatchett, Mike Hatchett, 1992.

E. All Guns Blazing 13a★★★★
Stick clip, 5 bolts, crux 1st to 2nd. A powerful bouldery start leads to "easier" 5.12 climbing. Lower off.
➤ Photo page 59.
FA: Dave Hatchett, Mike Hatchett, 1992.

F. Mudshark 13d★★
Stick clip, 7 bolts. Knee pads recommended for roof. Lower off.
FA: Joe Missick, Scott Burke, 1997.

G. Totally Chawsome 12b★★★★
Stick clip, 4 bolts, crux 2nd to 3rd. Bouldery start leads to undercling diagonal traverse to a technical reachy crux. Lower off. ➤ Photo page 61 and facing page.
FA: Dimitri Barton, Dave Hatchett, Mike Hatchett, 1990.

Mike Ossofsky on **Pow Wow** 11a****. ©*Jim Kovacs Photo.*

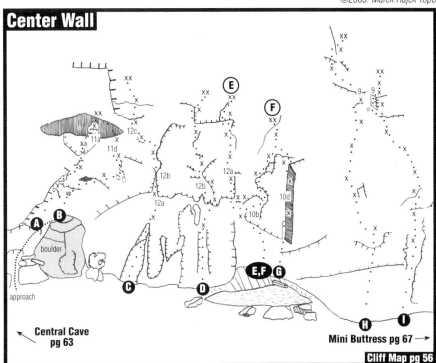

Center Wall

Big Chief Intro: Page 48. Sun hits this area after 12:30 P.M.

A. Pow Wow 11a★★★★
4 bolts, crux 3rd to 4th. Short but sweet overhanging climbing. Reachy crux. Lower off. ➤ Photo facing page.
FA: Mike Hatchett, Dave Hatchett, Rick Lovelace, 1990.

B. Peace Pipe 11d★★★
3 bolts, crux 1st to 3rd. Technical traverse followed by a bouldery crux to a traverse along a roof. Lower off.
FA: Dave Hatchett, Mike Hatchett, Rick Lovelace, 1990.

C. Ghost Dance 12c★★★
Stick clip, 6 bolts crux 1st to 3rd and 4th to 5th. Start up directly below and slightly left of the first bolt. Bouldery moves lead up to a powerful undercling, followed by difficult, sustained, overhanging climbing. Lower off.
FA: Mike Carville, 1995.

D. Scalper 12b★★★★★
Stick clip, 6 bolts crux 3rd to 4th. Overhanging face, through a tricky crux dihedral with a scalper sharp pocket, leads to an easier but sustained finish. Lower off.
FA: Dave Hatchett, Rick Lovelace.

E. Raindance 12a★★★★★
Stick clip, 6 bolts crux 3rd to 4th. Shares first bolt with *Mohawk*. Great sustained climbing up an overhanging face. Strenuous crux. Lower off.
FA: Dave Hatchett, Mike Hatchett, Rick Lovelace.

F. Mohawk 10b★★★★
Stick clip, 5 bolts, crux getting to 1st bolt! Very overhanging climbing along a sharp flake. Lower off.
➤ Photo page 66.
FA: Dave Hatchett, Jim Zellers, 7/1990.

G. Witch Doctor 10d★★★
4 bolts, crux 1st to 2nd. Crimpy edges inside a dihedral. Lower off.
FA: Mike Hatchett, Dave Hatchett, Rick Lovelace, 8/1990.

H. Warpath 9★★★★★
8 bolts, crux 6th to 7th. Use long slings on first 2 bolts to avoid rope drag. Jug haul up a steep face. Classic warm up. Lower off.
FA: Dave Hatchett, Mike Hatchett, 7/1990.

I. Warpaint 9★★★★
9 bolts, crux 7th to 8th. Positive hand holds. Awkward bulge at crux. Lower off.

See Page 65

Trang Hajek on **Mohawk** 10b****. ©*Jim Kovacs Photo.*

Mini Buttress

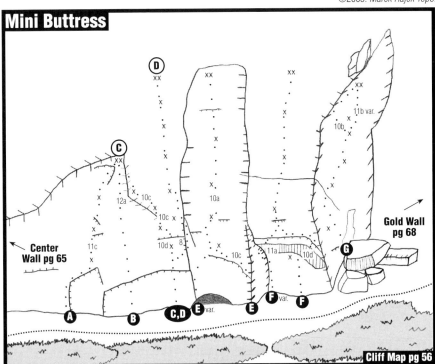

Center Wall pg 65
Gold Wall pg 68
Cliff Map pg 56

Mini Buttress

Big Chief Intro: Page 48. Sun hits this area after 12:30 P.M.

A. Eat the Worm 11c***
3 bolts, crux 1st to 2nd. Small edges and pinches. Short but good route. Lower off.
FA: Dave Hatchett, Jeff McKitterick, 1991.

B. Early Bird 12a**(tr)
Small sharp edges up steep face. Setup toprope from one of the two adjacent routes that share the same anchor.
FTR: Dave Hatchett, Jeff McKitterick.

C. Bird of Prey 10d***
4 bolts, crux 1st to 4th. Crimpers to sustained strenuous climbing. Lower off.

D. Wampum 8***
6 bolts, crux at 1st. A wide hand jam guards the access to easier climbing up a low angled face with nice edges. Lower off.

E. Route Stealers From Hell 10c***(R, 7)
4 bolts, crux getting to 1st bolt and 2nd to 3rd. Start on bouldery section right of bolt line or go up *Wampum* to first bolt for an easier start (route is 10a this way). Use a long sling on the 4th bolt to reduce rope drag. Runout from 4th bolt to anchor. Lower off.
FA: Dave Hatchett, Jeff McKitterick, 1992.

F. Force Feed 10d***
Stick clip, 4 bolts, crux 1st to 2nd. Start up small edges, then make a move right to jugs. Rope drag over bulge. Lower off.
FA: Dave Hatchett, Jeff McKitterick, 1991.
Variation: 11a***(R, 11a). Stick clip, 4 bolts, crux 1st to 2nd. Sharp edges along dihedral lead to jugs and a bulge. Rope drag over bulge. Lower off. Best done as a toprope.
FA: Dave Hatchett, Jeff McKitterick, 1991.

G. Too Light to Wait 10b***
5 bolts, crux 4th to 5th. Start on top of boulder. Traverse left toward 1st bolt. Climb left of bolt line at the top for 10b moves. Climbing is harder right of bolt line. Optionally, clip 1st bolt, step down and do hard direct start (11b), straight up face on nice edges. Lower off.
FA: Dave Hatchett, Jeff McKitterick, 1993.

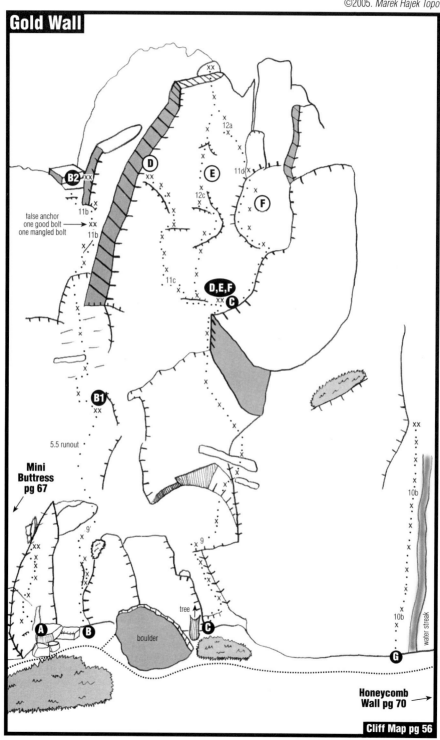

Gold Wall

B2

xx

D

E

11d

F

false anchor
one good bolt → xx
one mangled bolt

11b

11b

12a

12c

11c

D,E,F

C

B1

xx

5.5 runout

Mini
Buttress
pg 67

9'

xx

9

tree

A

B

boulder

C

10b

water streak

10b

G

Honeycomb
Wall pg 70 →

Cliff Map pg 56

Gold Wall

Big Chief Intro: Page 48. Sun hits this area around noon.

A. Too Light to Wait 10b★★★

5 bolts, crux 4th to 5th. Start on top of boulder. Traverse left toward 1st bolt. Climb left of bolt line at the top for 10b moves. Climbing is harder right of bolt line. Optionally, clip 1st bolt, step down and do hard direct start (11b), straight up face on nice edges. Lower off.
FA: Dave Hatchett, Jeff McKitterick, 1993.

B. Trail of Tears 11b★★★

Pitch 1: 9★★★(R, 5). 4 bolts, crux at 4th. Start 25' left of a large boulder. Mix of face and crack climbing at the bottom. Go right after the 4th bolt and climb around a steep headwall. Once past the headwall, stay a bit left where the climbing becomes very easy but extremely runout (5.5). Lower off or climb 2nd pitch. ☞ There are plans to add 3 bolts to this pitch, but it has not been done as of this printing.
FA: John Fox.

Pitch 2: 11b★★(R, 11a). 8 bolts, crux 7th to 8th. Pitch is constantly runout! Big scare factor on this pitch even for 5.12 climbers. Blocky face climbing followed by a crack leads to a large ledge. After getting to the 2nd bolt off of the ledge, head right into a dihedral for some stemming. The left hand variation is runout at 11b. Pass a false anchor (one bolt is mangled) and continue to the last bolt, head left around a corner to reach the anchor. 32m/105' pitch.
FA: John Fox.

C. This Toilet Earth 9★★★

12 bolts, crux at 4th. Approach from the left side of a large boulder, hike behind the boulder past a tree. Start in a dihedral. Climb to a small roof, diverse face climbing follows to a ledge. 45m/150' double rope rappel.
FA: Dave Hatchett, Jeff McKitterick, 1993.

The following three routes are all approached by climbing "This Toilet Earth". Descend via a 45m/150' rappel.

D. Gold Digger 11c★★★★

9 bolts, crux 2nd to 3rd. From the anchor of *This Toilet Earth* traverse left under a small roof. Keep traversing left through a balancy, crimpy crux to positive, pumpy holds. Very sustained, awesome climbing up a gently overhanging face. Leader should unclip bolt #3 when lowering to reduce potential pendulum for follower.
FA: Dave Hatchett, Mike Hatchett, 1991.

E. Copper Feather 12c★★(R, 12a)

9 bolts, crux 5th to 6th. From the anchor of *This Toilet Earth* traverse left under a small roof to the first bolt. Then up to a difficult mantle on a small, long ledge. Next, thin edges up overhanging face. Say goodbye to your fingertips. This is the most runout route at Big Chief. The rock is a bit loose. Tenuous finish. 30m/100' lower off.
FA: Todd Worsfold, 4/1990.

F. Golden Arch 12a★★★

9 bolts, opt. gear to 4" before 1st bolt, crux 7th to 8th. From the anchor of *This Toilet Earth* climb right along a crack to the first bolt. Next head left and up. Layback a right arching corner to a small roof, followed by very thin face climbing. Tenuous finish. Lower off.

G. Burning Toes 10b★★

10 bolts, crux 1st to 2nd and 7th to 8th. Delicate, balancy climbing on thin edges. A bit loose and dirty. This will be an awesome route once it cleans up. Located about 100' right of *This Toilet Earth*, past a cluster of water streaks. There is a lichen/water streak just right of the bolt line.

©2005. Marek Hajek Topo.

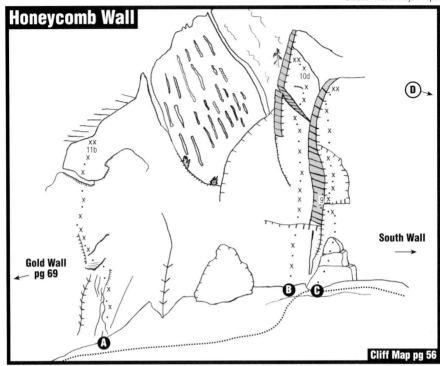

Honeycomb Wall

Big Chief Intro: Page 48. In the summer this crag comes into the sun around noon.

A. Dogfight 11b★★★★

9 bolts, crux 9th to anchor. Climb a crack to a ledge, then to a thin crimpy face, to a steep technical reachy finish. Lower off. ➤ Photo page 2.
FA: Dave Hatchett, Jeff McKitterick.

B. Sweating Bullets 10d★★★★

12 bolts, crux 11th to 12th. Climb a face to a big ledge, then climb easy jugs to progressively harder and smaller holds. Finish on overhanging face with a few crack moves. Lower off.
FA: Dave Hatchett, Jeff McKitterick.

C. Times Up 9★★★★

7 bolts, crux 2nd to 3rd. At the 2nd bolt climb left of arete, after a couple moves up, traverse right to the 3rd bolt, or climb a reachy thin crux straight up arete and then right (10b). Lower off.
FA: Dave Hatchett, Jeff McKitterick.

D. Project ?

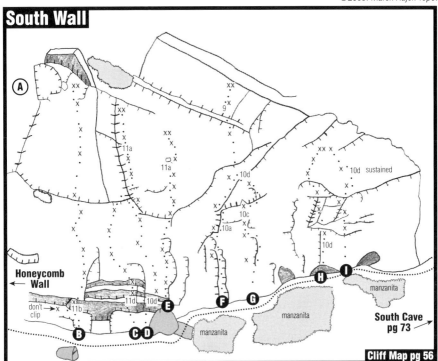

South Wall
Big Chief Intro: Page 48. In summer this crag comes into the sun at noon.

A. Open Project ?
The proposed name for this line was *Sweathog*. The project was abandoned. Feel free to finish it.
P: Dave Hatchett.

B. Drill Drop 11b★★★
Stick clip, 9 bolts, crux before first bolt. Stick clip the bolt near the first small ledge. Don't clip the lone bolt below the roof on the left. Blocky, bouldery start to varied cerebral face climbing. Lower off.
FA: Dave Hatchett, Brian Mason, 10/1990.

C. Live Wire 11d★★★
Stick clip, 9 bolts, crux before first bolt. Strenuous roof and crack followed by a balancy move to face. Nice rest ledge half way up. Finish on crimpy, thin face. Lower off.
FA: Chris Bauman, Dave Hatchett, 11/1990.

D. Pain Killer 11a★★★★
Stick clip, 8 bolts, crux 7th to 8th. Tall people can climb on top of the boulder at the base of the route and clip from there. Start left of the boulder. Climb through an overhanging blocky section to face, then traverse left underneath a roof with stunningly incut holds to a good rest ledge. Finish on crimpy, thin face. Lower off.
➤ Photo page 73.
FA: Dave Hatchett, Rick Lovelace, 6/1990.

E. May Cause Dizzyness 11a★★★
9 bolts, crux at 7th. Start on top of the boulder. Face climb to a small roof followed by thin, crimpy face. A small hole in the rock awaits you just past the crux. Lower off.
FA: Dave Hatchett, Jeff McKitterick, 1992.

F. Festus 10a★★★★
6 bolts, crux 2nd to 3rd and at 6th. Climb toward a right arching corner. A reachy crux awaits at the bottom of the corner. Climb to diagonal crack then to face. I am told that the reachy crux feels more like 10d for short people. Lower off. ➤ Photo pages 14, 82.
FA: Brian Mason, Dave Hatchett, 10/1990.

G. May Cause Drowsiness 10d★★★★
7 bolts, crux 3rd to 4th and 5th to 6th. Start 15 feet right of *Festus* in line with a right facing corner. A thin crux leads to a short traverse to the right, then to a reachy crux move. Route merges with *Festus* at that point. Lower off.
FA: Dave Hatchett, Brian Mason, 10/1990.

H. Glass Eye 10d★★
Stick clip, 5 bolts, crux getting to 1st. Overhanging dihedral to face. Lower off.
FA: Dave Hatchett, Jeff McKitterick, 1993.

I. Donkey Show 10d★★
Stick clip, 5 bolts, crux 4th to anchor. Juggy, overhanging start to face. Lower off.
FA: Dave Hatchett, Jeff McKitterick, 1993.

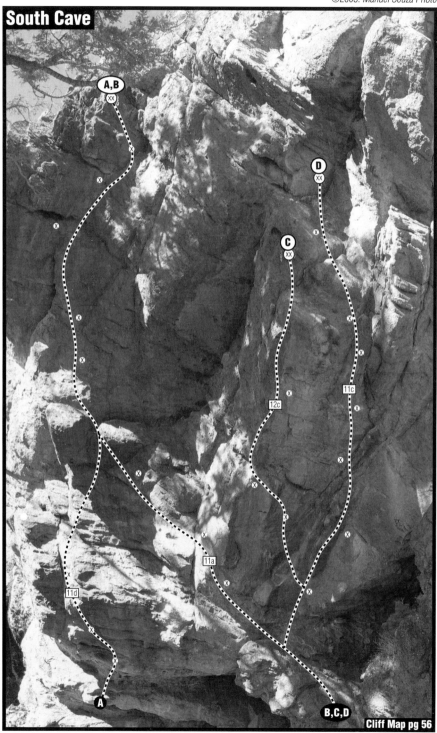

South Cave

A,B
XX

D
XX

C
XX

12c

11c

11a

11d

A

B,C,D

Cliff Map pg 56

Chris Kurrle on **Pain Killer** 11a****. ©*Jim Kovacs Photo.*

See Page 71

©2005. *Marty Lewis Topo.*

South Cave

Big Chief Intro: Page 48. Receives sun for a brief period of time around noon, then goes back into shade.

A. Realm of the Overhang Variation 11d**
8 bolts, crux 2nd to 3rd. A strenuous and bouldery direct start to *Realm of the Overhang.* Lower off.
FA: Dave Hatchett, Mike Hatchett, 1991.

B. Realm of the Overhang 11a***
8 bolts, crux 1st to 2nd. A reachy crux around corner to sustained climbing along crack inside dihedral. Lower off.
FA: Dave Hatchett, Mike Hatchett, 1991.

C. Lousiana Lip Lock 12c**
4 bolts, crux 3rd to 4th. Very overhanging reachy climb. Start on face, traverse left then up along overhanging arete.

D. Flying High Again 11c****
7 bolts, crux 4th to 5th. Slopey holds along right facing corner to an overhanging, technical crux.
FA: Dave Hatchett, Hidetaka Suzuki.

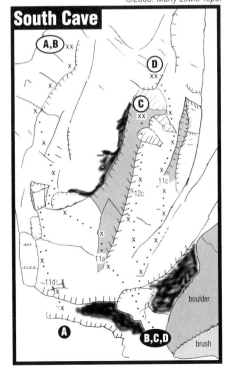

South Cave

Cliff Map pg 56

Upper Backside

Big Chief Intro: Page 48. These routes are best climbed in the late afternoon in the summer, when this crag goes into the shade.

A. Sandblaster Arete 12b***

9 bolts, crux 3rd to 4th. Great holds on an overhanging arete. Very abrasive rock! Lower off.
FA: Dave Hatchett, 1992.

B. Jungle Preacher 11b***

8 bolts, crux 3rd to 4th. Traverse two overhanging corners. Sustained. Good holds. Abrasive rock! Use long draw on the 3rd bolt to lessen rope drag. Lower off.
FA: Dave Hatchett, Dave Griffith, 1992.

C. Jr. Knows Best 11c*(tr)

Face. Dirty. Somebody, please bolt and clean up this face. Difficult to top-rope.

Lower Backside

Cliff Map pg 56

Lower Backside

Big Chief Intro: Page 48. These routes are best climbed in the late afternoon in the summer, when this crag goes into the shade.

A. The Accused 11b**

9 bolts, crux 2nd to 3rd. Starts on a right leaning ramp that leads to a vertical demarcation between light and dark rock to get to the 1st bolt. Face with edges and sidepulls towards obvious dishes. A bit dirty. Use longer draws on first three bolts to reduce rope drag. Lower off.
FA: Dave Hatchett, Sean Sullivan, 1993.

B. Morning Sweater 11c·

4 bolts, crux 3rd to 4th. Scramble up a blocky gully just right of a large rotten hole, then move left on a sloping shelf to reach the 1st bolt, finish on extremely sharp edges up a slightly overhanging face. A bit loose and dirty. Lower off.
FA: Joe Missick, Mike Eadington, 1992.

C. Countdown 11a*

5 bolts, crux at 1st and 3rd to 4th. Starts on the right edge of the buttress. Sharp thin edges up a steep face. Gritty. Lower off.
FA: Will Jones, 1992.

©2005. *Marek Hajek Photo.*

South Buttress
Left Side

Right Side ⟶

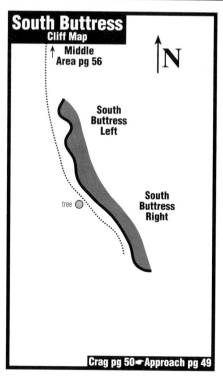

South Buttress
Cliff Map

↑ **Middle**
Area pg 56

↑N

South Buttress Left

tree ○

South Buttress Right

Crag pg 50 ☛ **Approach pg 49**

South Buttress - Left

Big Chief Intro: Page 48. Southern-most crag at Big Chief. South of the South Pass. In the summer this crag comes into the sun by noon.

A. Aunt Martha's Mustache 11(tr)

Loose and dirty. Somebody, please bolt this face and clean up the climb.
P: Dave Hatchett, Mike Hatchett.

B. Sugar Fix 10d★★★

7 bolts, crux 4th to 5th. This climb starts inside a right facing dihedral followed by balancy climbing up a blocky face. A set of bouldery moves between blocks. Lower off.
FA: Dave Hatchett, Mike Hatchett.

C. 7-11 Burrito 10a★★★

9 bolts, crux 4th to 5th and 8th to 9th. Start up a steep right facing ramp to a short dihedral. Finish on a thin, technical face. Lower off.
FA: Dave Hatchett, Mike Hatchett.

D. Slurpee Headache 11a★★★

Stick clip, 9 bolts, crux getting to 1st. Start 10' to the right of *7-11 Burrito*. Climb up overhanging face past a small roof to a thin, technical face. Lower off.
FA: Dave Hatchett, Mike Hatchett.

©2005. *Marek Hajek Photo.*

South Buttress
Right Side

South Buttress - Right

A. Junk Food Junkie 10c★★★
9 bolts, crux 3rd to 5th and 8th to 9th. This route is located near the most prominent evergreen tree at roughly the center of the cliff. Begin by climbing towards a left facing corner 15' off the ground. At the top of the corner climb a technical crux to thin, technical face climbing. Lower off.
FA: Dave Hatchett, Mike Hatchett.

B. Glass Moon 12a★
6 bolts, crux 3rd to 5th. Start 10' right of *Junk Food Junkie*. Blocky face to sharp abrasive edges. Rock is covered by lichen. Lower off.
FA: Dave Hatchett, Mike Hatchett.

C. Quick Stop 12a★
7 bolts, crux at 2nd. Crimpy headwall to lichen covered corner system to arete. Abrasive rock. Reachy crux at 2nd bolt. Lower off.
FA: Dave Hatchett, Mike Hatchett.

D. Milking a Dead Cow 13a?★★
6 bolts, crux 3rd to 4th. Overhanging arete. Lower off.
☞ I have not been able to objectively rate this route because I can't make the crux move, seems way harder than the original 12c rating. Feedback is appreciated.
FA: Dave Hatchett, Mike Hatchett.

E. Community Service 10b★★
3 bolts, crux 2nd to 3rd. The right most route at the South Buttress. Balancy dihedral climbing. Lower off.
FA: Dave Hatchett, Mike Hatchett.

See Page 81

Marek Hajek on the **Unforgiven** 10a**. ©*Pete Dronkers Photo.*

Adapted from the U.S.G.S. 1:24,000 Tahoe City.

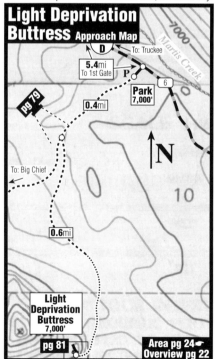

Light Deprivation Buttress Approach Map

To: Truckee

5.4mi
To 1st Gate

**Park
7,000'**

0.4mi

pg 79

To: Big Chief

0.6mi

**Light
Deprivation
Buttress
7,000'**

pg 81

Area pg 24
Overview pg 22

Light Deprivation Buttress

Elevation: 7,000 ft.
Exposure: Southwest facing.
Sport Climbs: 9 routes, 5.9 to 12c.
Approach: 20 minute hike.

Light Deprivation Buttress

This small formation is southwest facing and receives sun until about 2:30 P.M. In the heat of the summer this crag offers pleasant late afternoon climbing. There are two formations 30 feet apart, the main cliff and a large boulder named the Hershey Kiss Boulder. One can easily spend the whole day climbing at this area.

The cliff hosts several excellent routes. The rock is somewhat abrasive. The Hershey Kiss Boulder hosts several short, pleasant routes on the south and west faces. One can easily scramble to the top of the boulder from the east side to setup topropes.

The Approach: See *Getting There* page 23. At 5.4 miles past the first gate on Forest Service Rd. #6 look for a plowed-over logging road on the right side. Fifty feet past this road is another road on the right that will take you directly to the "Big Chief parking lot." Typically, there is a cairn at the entrance. Please, park responsibly so that others can find space as well.

From the Big Chief Parking Area, follow the Big Chief logging road for about 0.4 miles to a junction. Here the road widens into a triangular clearing with an old fire pit. A small, windy logging road veers off left. Follow this windy road for about 0.4 miles on fairly level ground. The road turns into a

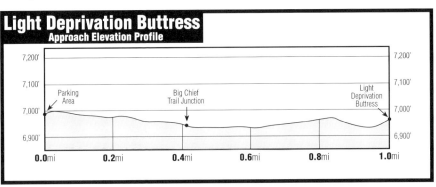

trail. Stay on the trail for another 0.2 miles. Toward the end, the trail becomes faint. Continue in the direction traveled and skirt along the left side of a rock formation.

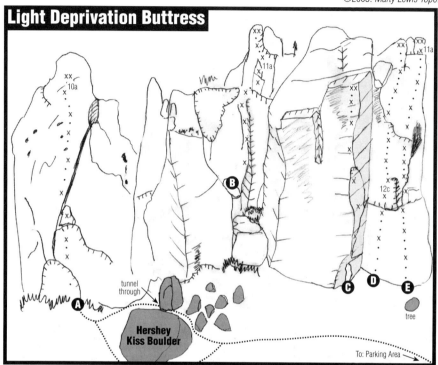

Light Deprivation Buttress
Intro: Page 78.

A. Una-Bomber 10a★★★
8 bolts, crux 8th to anchor. Face and arete. Reachy crux is more like 10d for shorter people. Lower off.
FA: Dave Hatchett, Mike Hatchett.

B. Night Stalker 11a★★★★
9 bolts, crux 7th to 8th. Arete to face. One of the few routes here with non-abrasive rock. Lower off.
FA: Dave Hatchett, Mike Hatchett.

C. Infra-Red 9★★★
6 bolts. Start inside dihedral with a crack, then around arete to pockets on steep face. Lower off.
FA: Will Jones, Dave Hatchett.

D. Shot in the Dark 12c★★
9 bolts, crux at 3rd. Thin face followed by a bouldery move to fun, easy pockets. Abrasive rock. Lower off.
FA: Dave Hatchett, Mike Hatchett.

E. Shadow Dancer 11a★★★★
11 bolts, crux 11th to anchor. Awesome, sustained climb! Corner to face to bulge. Abrasive rock. Lower off.
FA: Will Jones, Dave Hatchett.

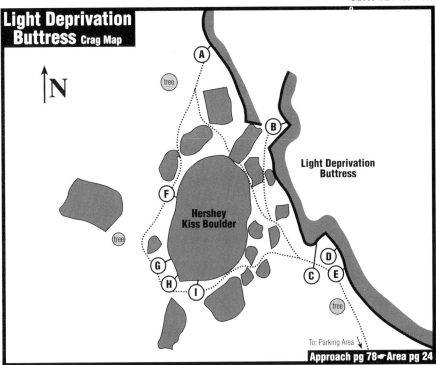

Light Deprivation Buttress Crag Map

↑N

Light Deprivation
Buttress

Hershey
Kiss Boulder

To: Parking Area

Approach pg 78 ☞ Area pg 24

Hershey Kiss Boulder

boulder

brush

F,G,H

Hershey Kiss Boulder
This large boulder is right below the Light Deprivation Buttress.

F. Allegro 10d★★
5 bolts, crux 2nd to 3rd. Slab climbing through a roof. Use long draws on first two bolts. Lower off.

G. Fade to Black 9★★★
4 bolts, crux 3rd to 4th. Bowl shaped holds up face. Finish on arete. Lower off.
FA: Dave Hatchett, Mike Hatchett.

H. Funtastic 10c★★
6 bolts, crux at 1st. Arete. Lower off.

I. Unforgiven 10a★★
4 bolts, crux at 2nd. Slabby face, crack past the roof. Lower off. ➤ Photo page 78.

See Page 71
Trang Hajek on **Festus** 10a**** at Big Chief. ©*Jim Kovacs Photo.*

Big Chief. ©*Pete Dronkers Photo.*

CHAPTER 4

APPENDIX

Recreational Activities

So you're on a road trip, and now after climbing at Big Chief for several days straight you are wondering what to do on your days off. That is certainly a loaded topic. You are visiting not only the premier sport climbing area in the Tahoe region, you are also visiting a premier playground. Whether you enjoy backpacking, beach volleyball, flying in small planes, golf, hiking, horseback riding, hot air balloon rides, kayaking, mountain biking, parasailing, scuba diving, skiing, snow shoeing, water skiing, white water rafting, or just lounging on the beach the Truckee/Lake Tahoe region has it all.

Truckee has some great resources that deserve your visit.

The Sports Exchange (see advertisement on page 6), located close to the Big Chief entrance, sells climbing supplies and rents climbing shoes, kayaks, mountain bikes, skis, snow boards, snow shoes and has knowledgeable staff that can help you pick an activity.

The Truckee Ranger District has a wealth of information on camping and hiking. See map page 26 or see page 19 for contact information.

The Truckee Chamber of Commerce has lots of contacts for various businesses that offer tours and other recreational activities. Visit their website www.truckee.com or stop by at 10065 Donner Pass Rd. Phone (530) 587-2757.

The internet these days yields a wealth of information. A search for Truckee and your favorite activity will provide lots of information.

Author's Recommendations

Are you on a road trip planning to visit just once or visiting for the first time and would like an agenda? Here are a few recommendations:

For all levels, Circuit #1 is roughly south to north. Circuit #2 is roughly north to south. Routes are listed in order to provide a warm up and cool down. The nature of the routes is taken into account.

Level 5.10

Circuit 1		Circuit 2	
❏ Times Up 9	70	❏ Sundance 10a	55
❏ Festus 10a	71	❏ Halfbaked 10c	55
❏ Warpaint 9	65	❏ Flame Thrower 10d	56
❏ Warpath 9	65	❏ Mohawk 10b	65
❏ Mohawk 10b	65	❏ Too Light to Wait 10b	67
❏ Too Light to Wait 10b	67	❏ Sweating Bullets 10d	70
❏ Flame Thrower 10d	56	❏ Times Up 9	70
❏ Sundance 10a	55	❏ Festus 10a	71

Level 5.11

Circuit 1		Circuit 2	
❏ Times Up 9	70	❏ Sundance 10a	55
❏ Festus 10a	71	❏ Halfbaked 10c	55
❏ Sweating Bullets 10d	70	❏ Undercooked 11b	55
❏ May Cause Dizzyness 11a	71	❏ Pow Wow 11a	65
❏ Pain Killer 11a	71	❏ Dog Fight 11b	70
❏ Flying High Again 11c	73	❏ May Cause Dizzyness 11a	71
❏ Pow Wow 11b	65	❏ Flying High Again 11c	73
❏ Mohawk 10b	65	❏ Festus 10a	71

Level 5.12

Circuit 1		Circuit 2	
❏ Festus 10a	71	❏ Sundance 10a	55
❏ Sweating Bullets 10d	70	❏ Halfbaked 10c	55
❏ Dog Fight 11b	70	❏ Undercooked 11b	55
❏ Flying High Again 11c	73	❏ Eye of the Beholder 11d	56
❏ Raindance 12a	65	❏ Raindance 12a	65
❏ Scalper 12b	65	❏ Scalper 12b	65
❏ Totally Chawsome 12b	63	❏ Totally Chawsome 12b	63
❏ Wicked Quickie 12d	63	❏ Wicked Quickie 12d	63
❏ Pow Wow 11a	65	❏ Pow Wow 11a	65
❏ Mohawk 10b	65	❏ Mohawk 10b	65

Level 5.13

Circuit 1		Circuit 2	
❏ Festus 10a	71	❏ Halfbaked 10c	55
❏ Sweating Bullets 10d	70	❏ Undercooked 11b	55
❏ Flying High Again 11c	73	❏ Pow Wow 11a	65
❏ Raindance 12a	65	❏ Raindance 12a	65
❏ Totally Chawsome 12b	63	❏ Totally Chawsome 12b	63
❏ All Guns Blazing 13a	63	❏ All Guns Blazing 13a	63
❏ Mudshark 13d	63	❏ Mudshark 13d	63
❏ Pow Wow 11a	65	❏ Pow Wow 11a	65
❏ Mohawk 10b	65	❏ Mohawk 10b	65

ROUTES BY RATING

7***
❏ Hunchy Bunchy Banana Pants   42

8***
❏ Wampum   67

9**
❏ Jimmy   42

9***
❏ Fade to Black   81
❏ Infra-Red   80
❏ This Toilet Earth   69
❏ Trail of Tears (1ˢᵗ pitch)   69

9****
❏ Times Up   70
❏ Warpaint   65

9*****
❏ Warpath   65

10a·
❏ Livestock Pasture   59

10a**
❏ North Pillar   52
❏ Unforgiven   81

10a***
❏ 7-11 Burrito   76
❏ Sundance   55
❏ Una-Bomber   80

10a****
❏ Festus   71
❏ Pollo Del Fuego   42

10b*
❏ Laas Rocket   53
❏ Lemmiwinks   38

10b**
❏ Burning Toes   69
❏ Community Service   77
❏ Lost Souls   59

10b***
❏ Sunshine   55
❏ Too Light to Wait   67

10b****
❏ Mohawk   65
❏ Skimmy   42

10c**
❏ Funambulist   61
❏ Funtastic   81
❏ Geranium   39
❏ Pickled Pigs Feet   38

10c***
❏ Halfbaked   55
❏ Junk Food Junkie   77
❏ Route Stealers From Hell   56

10c****
❏ Pre-emptive Strike   44

10d*
❏ Green Hornet (1ˢᵗ pitch)   59
❏ Green Hornet (2ⁿᵈ pitch)   59
❏ Kalumet Arete (1ˢᵗ pitch)   59

10d**
❏ Allegro   81
❏ Donkey Show   77
❏ Glass Eye   77
❏ Thrash Under Pressure   59

10d***
❏ Bird of Prey   67
❏ Force Feed   67
❏ Killer Bee   63
❏ Sugar Fix   76
❏ Travail Buttress   55
❏ Witch Doctor   65

10d****
❏ Flame Thrower   56
❏ May Cause Drowsiness   77
❏ Sixteen Virgins   45
❏ Sweating Bullets   70

10d*****
❏ Threat Level Orange   44

12a*
❏ Glass Moon 77
❏ Quick Stop 77

12a**
❏ Early Bird (tr) 67
❏ Medicine Man 55
❏ Shit List 38

12a***
❏ Golden Arch 69
❏ Weapons of Mass Destruction 45

12a*****
❏ Lord Braggart 43
❏ Raindance 65

12b*
❏ Jeronimo 53

12b**
❏ Freak of Nature 55

12b***
❏ Sandblaster Arete 74

12b****
❏ Totally Chawsome 63

12b*****
❏ Scalper 65

12c·
❏ Jeronimo Drinking Fire Water 53

12c**
❏ Copper Feather 69
❏ Lousiana Lip Lock 73
❏ Shot in the Dark 80

12c***
❏ Ghost Dance 65

12d·
❏ Firewater 53

12d***
❏ Climb Against Nature 55
❏ Wicked Quickie 63

13a·
❏ Crackle 55

13a**
❏ Milking a Dead Cow 77

13a****
❏ All Guns Blazing 63

13b***
❏ Blazing Buckets 63

13c**
❏ Vulgar Display of Power 63

13d**
❏ Mudshark 63

Unknown
❏ Aunt Martha's Mustache 11(tr) 76
❏ Spider Hole 45
❏ Shock & Awe 45

INDEX

U

V

W

X

Y

Z

The Author fact checking at Big Chief. ©*Jim Kovacs Photo.*

ABOUT THE AUTHOR

Marek Hajek grew up in the Czech Republic, the city of Budweiser (České Budějovice). At the age of 13 he came to Berwyn, Illinois where he went to high school and learned English. In 1989 he moved to Lake Tahoe and has stayed in the area ever since.

In 1992, Don Harder introduced Marek to rock climbing at Donner Summit on a climb named *Escargot* (11a). After a ten-minute struggle and many rope hangs later, Marek lowered down from the first bolt with a vicious flash pump. Don continued to dish out such abuse for many months to come, perhaps in hopes of dwindling the climbing population by discouragement.

Progress through the grades came very slowly for Marek. After a couple of years of climbing he finally redpointed his first 5.9. The 5.10s seemed beyond reach, the 5.11s impossible and the 5.12s for the climbing gods. Marek worked his way through the grades one letter grade at a time over many years. Through persistence, he managed to climb and reclimb all but three routes at Big Chief. In 2003, during a layoff from a startup company, Marek decided to put together an updated, stand alone guide to Big Chief.

After graduating from the University of Nevada, Reno in 1998 with an electrical engineering degree Marek met Trang at his first job. Trang received an introduction to rock climbing on their first date, 200 feet away from *Escargot* on a slightly easier climb. For some strange reason she continued to date Marek and married him in the summer of 2001. They continue to live in Reno, Nevada and climb in the Lake Tahoe area.

About Maximus Press

Maximus Press was launched in 1990 with the publication of the pamphlet "<u>Owens River Gorge Climbs</u>". Garage-style in appearance, this publication was nevertheless accurate, concise and easy to use. Fifteen years later after considerable improvements, Maximus Press continues to strive to produce the most useful and state-of-the-art guidebooks possible. The knowledge base of our editorial staff comes from years of experience climbing, exploring and living in the Sierra Nevada Mountains. You can count on our commitment to deliver high-quality books.

—Marty Lewis
Publisher

Another shipment of books coming your way.

Guidebooks available from Maximus Press

Maximus Press Books can be found at fine outdoor shops or ordered directly. California residents please include 7.75% sales tax. Shipping and handling included in price. Prices subject to change without notice.

http://maximuspress.com

Maximus Press
P.O. Box 1565
Bishop, CA 93515
Phone & Fax: 760-387-1013
E-mail: smlewis@qnet.com

MAXIMVS PRESS

SPORT CLIMBING IN
THE SANTA MONICAS

by Louie Anderson

**SOUTHERN CALIFORNIA
CLIMBING GUIDES VOL. 1**

June 2003 - 2nd Edition
250 pages - $30.00
ISBN 0-9676116-6-0

The Climbing Guide to the
Santa Monica Mountains

• **Echo Cliffs**
• **Boney Bluff**
• **Malibu Creek**
• **Black Flower**
• **Tick Rock**
• **Conejo Mountain**

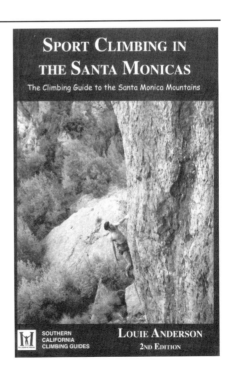

SPORT CLIMBING IN
THE SANTA MONICAS
The Climbing Guide to the Santa Monica Mountains

SOUTHERN
CALIFORNIA
CLIMBING GUIDES

LOUIE ANDERSON
2ND EDITION

Mammoth Area Rock Climbs

by Marty Lewis and John Moynier

EASTERN SIERRA CLIMBING GUIDES VOL. 2

May 2004 - 3rd Edition
288 pages - $30.00
ISBN 0-9676116-5-2

The Climbing Guide to the Eastern Sierra—North.

- **Rock Creek**
- **Benton Crags**
- **Bear Crag**
- **Clark Canyon**
- **Deadman's Bouldering**
- **Granite Basin**

The Good, the Great, and The Awesome

by Peter Croft

EASTERN SIERRA CLIMBING GUIDES VOL. 4

July 2002 - 1st Edition
244 pages - $30.00
ISBN 0-9676116-4-4

The Guidebook to the Top 40 High Sierra Rock Climbs

- **Tricks of the Trade**
- **Whitney Region**
- **Palisades**
- **Bishop High Country**
- **Tuolumne Meadows**
- **Roadside Cragging**